CHINESE STATE-OWNED ENTERPRISES AND U.S.-CHINA BILATERAL INVESTMENT

I0447562

HEARING

BEFORE THE

U.S.-CHINA ECONOMIC AND SECURITY

REVIEW COMMISSION

ONE HUNDRED TWELFTH CONGRESS

FIRST SESSION

_____

MARCH 30, 2011

_____

Printed for use of the
United States-China Economic and Security Review Commission
Available via the World Wide Web: www.uscc.gov

UNITED STATES-CHINA ECONOMIC AND SECURITY REVIEW COMMISSION

WASHINGTON :   2011

U.S.-CHINA ECONOMIC AND SECURITY REVIEW COMMISSION

The Commission was created on October 30, 2000 by the Floyd D. Spence National Defense Authorization Act for 2001 § 1238, Public Law No. 106-398, 114 STAT. 1654A-334 (2000) (codified at 22 U.S.C.§ 7002 (2001), as amended by the Treasury and General Government Appropriations Act for 2002 § 645 (regarding employment status of staff) & § 648 (regarding changing annual report due date from March to June), Public Law No. 107-67, 115 STAT. 514 (Nov. 12, 2001); as amended by Division P of the "Consolidated Appropriations Resolution, 2003," Pub L. No. 108-7 (Feb. 20, 2003) (regarding Commission name change, terms of Commissioners, and responsibilities of Commission); as amended by Public Law No. 109-108 (H.R. 2862) (Nov. 22, 2005) (regarding responsibilities of Commission and applicability of FACA); as amended by Division J of the "Consolidated Appropriations Act, 2008," Public Law No. 110-161 (December 26, 2007) (regarding responsibilities of the Commission, and changing the Annual Report due date from June to December).

The Commission's full charter is available at www.uscc.gov.

April 5, 2011

The Honorable Daniel Inouye
President Pro Tempore of the Senate, Washington, D.C. 20510
The Honorable John A. Boehner
Speaker of the House of Representatives, Washington, D.C. 20515

DEAR SENATOR INOUYE AND SPEAKER BOEHNER:

We are pleased to notify you of our March 30, 2011 public hearing on *"Chinese State-Owned Enterprises and U.S.-China Bilateral Investment."* The Floyd D. Spence National Defense Authorization Act (amended by Pub. L. No. 109-108, section 635(a)) provides the basis for this hearing.

At the hearing, the Commissioners heard from the following witnesses: Dr. Barry J. Naughton, Dr. Derek Scissors, Dr. Theodore H. Moran, Dr. Robert E. Scott, Dr. K.C. Fung, Mr. Daniel H. Rosen, and Dr. Karl P. Sauvant. The subjects covered included the nature and activities of state-owned enterprises in the People's Republic of China as well as the patterns and implications of bilateral investment between the United States and China.

We note that the full transcript of the hearing will be posted to the Commission's website when completed. The prepared statements and supporting documents submitted by the participants are now posted on the Commission's website at www.uscc.gov. Members and the staff of the Commission are available to provide more detailed briefings. We hope these materials will be helpful to the Congress as it continues its assessment of U.S.-China relations and their impact on U.S. security.

The Commission will examine in greater depth these issues, and the other issues enumerated in its statutory mandate, in its 2011 Annual Report that will be submitted to Congress in November 2011. Should you have any questions regarding this hearing or any other issue related to China, please do not hesitate to have your staff contact our Congressional Liaison, Jonathan Weston, at 202-624-1487 or jweston@uscc.gov.

Sincerely yours,

William A. Reinsch
Chairman

Daniel M. Slane
Vice Chairman

CONTENTS

WEDNESDAY, MARCH 30, 2011

CHINESE STATE-OWNED ENTERPRISES AND U.S.-CHINA BILATERAL INVESTMENT

PANEL I: CONGRESSIONAL PERSPECTIVES

PANEL II: STATE-OWNED ENTERPRISES IN CHINA

PANEL III: U.S. INVESTMENTS IN CHINA

PANEL IV: CHINEST INVESTMENTS IN THE UNITED STATES

ADDITIONAL MATERIAL SUBMITTED FOR THE RECORD

CHINESE STATE-OWNED ENTERPRISES AND U.S.-CHINA BILATERAL INVESTMENT

WEDNESDAY, MARCH 30, 2011

───────────────

U.S.-CHINA ECONOMIC AND SECURITY REVIEW COMMISSION

Washington, D.C.

The Commission met in Room 538 Dirksen Senate Office Building, Washington, D.C. at 8:55 a.m., Chairman William A. Reinsch, and Vice Chairman Daniel M. Slane and Michael R. Wessel (Hearing Co-Chairs), presiding.

OPENING STATEMENT OF COMMISSIONER MICHAEL R. WESSEL
HEARING CO-CHAIR

HEARING CO-CHAIR WESSEL: Let's go ahead and get started this morning, and we'll dispense with opening statements and appreciate Congresswoman DeLauro making her way over to this side of the Capitol to be with us this morning.

Congressman DeLauro represents Connecticut's 3rd Congressional District. She is a member of the House Appropriations Committee and the Ranking Member of the Subcommittee on Labor, Health and Human Services, Education and Related Agencies.

The Congresswoman has been a leader in the fight for food safety and has supported the restrictions on poultry imports from countries like China that have faced avian influenza.

The Congresswoman is also a strong advocate for American workers and is the sponsor of H. Res. 106, a bipartisan resolution expressing the House of Representatives' sense that the new presidential helicopter fleet should be built using products manufactured in America and that the Defense Department should prohibit any defense acquisition bid involving

1

any entity controlled, directed or influenced by the government of China.

Congresswoman, we're happy to have you with us today, for your long-standing friendship for this Commission and leadership on issues important not only to your state but working people all across the country.

[The written statement follows:]

PREPARED STATEMENT OF COMMISSIONER MICHAEL R. WESSEL
HEARING CO-CHAIR

Good morning and thank you for coming. Today's hearing on "Chinese State-Owned Enterprises and U.S.-China bilateral investments" is our fourth hearing of the year. I would like to thank Senator Sherrod Brown and his staff for helping to secure today's hearing venue.

For those who are new to our hearings, we are a bipartisan Congressionally-chartered Commission composed of 12 members, six of whom are selected by the Majority and Minority leaders of the Senate and six by the Speaker and the Minority Leader of the House.

Today's hearing will examine three aspects of China's economic policy. The first is China's state-owned or state-controlled companies and industries, which together constitute an estimated 30 to 40 percent of China's economy. These companies, generally the largest ones in China, are operated and managed by the central government of the People's Republic. They are an instrument of state power as well as the centerpiece of China's industrial policy. They receive massive government subsidies and are protected from competition from foreign companies. In addition, there are more than 100,000 smaller companies that are owned or operated by provincial and local governments. These companies also receive many benefits from their government ownership. Their persistence and their outsized influence in China certainly violate the spirit of the free market principles of the World Trade Organization.

All this is occurring just as our ability to address China's unfair trade practices is threatened by a decision from the World Trade Organization. Two weeks ago, the WTO issued a decision that attacks the vital ability of the United States to fight unfair Chinese subsidies. In addition, in just five years, China's official WTO designation as a non-market economy expires, further hobbling the U.S. ability to challenge China's unwillingness to embrace further economic reform.

These state-owned enterprises are increasingly active globally, seeking to expand China's economic opportunities and power around the globe. They're involved in aerospace, autos, oil, steel, telecommunications and numerous other industries.

As agents of the state, their activities demand enormous scrutiny as they come armed with support not only of their government, but with the trillions of dollars in financial reserves that the country has amassed.

But, we also need to understand what other Chinese entities are doing – not a simple task. Beyond the state-owned or state-invested enterprises, there are companies that act under the direction of the state or with delegated authority. We need to understand the implications of their efforts.

Two separate panels will examine U.S. direct investment in China and Chinese direct investment in the United States. Both forms of investment have been increasing, especially U.S. investment in China. As you will hear, more than half of the imports to the United States are from foreign invested enterprises in China.

We have some excellent witnesses today who are quite expert on these complex issues. I'd like to ask that each witness limit his remarks to just seven minutes in order to leave plenty of time for questions and answers. First, we will hear from Congresswoman Rosa DeLauro from Connecticut and when he is able to come, Congressman Maurice Hinchey from New York.

PANEL I: CONGRESSIONAL PERSPECTIVES

STATEMENT OF ROSA DELAURO
A U.S. REPRESENTATIVE FROM THE STATE OF CONNECTICUT

MS. DeLAURO: Thank you very much.

It's a real honor for me to be here this morning. It gave me an opportunity, as well, to come over to the Senate side, which I don't have too much opportunity to do. Though the House members usually come over to the Senate side, it's often not the case in reciprocity. But it's a delight to be here with you, and I thank you for the introduction.

I want to also say a thank you to Vice Chairman Slane and the Commissioners for holding what is a very important hearing on "Chinese State-Owned Enterprises and U.S.-China Bilateral Investment," and again it's an honor for me to be here this morning to testify.

I want to extend a thank you to my good friend, long-time friend, Commissioner Michael Wessel, a very helpful advisor over the years and resource on a number of issues for me over the years as a member.

The work that you do here at the Commission, and particularly the in-depth annual report that you put out, is critically important. We count on your expertise and insights to inform our work in the Congress as we seek to meet the economic and national security challenges posed by China.

I know today's hearing will examine a broad range of issues. I want to focus on a deep concern of mine and one that could have an impact on both my state of Connecticut and the nation at large, and that is China's advancements in the aerospace industry.

According to a report published last year by the Economic Policy Institute, between 2001, when China joined the World Trade Organization, and 2008, 2.4 million jobs were lost or displaced as a result of our trade deficit with China. This cost over 27,000 jobs in Connecticut alone.

In 1990, our trade deficit with China stood at just $10 billion, and in the two decades since, it has risen astronomically and is now estimated at $273 billion.

That trade deficit is a large driver of the crisis in domestic manufacturing that we now face here at home. The erosion of our manufacturing base has, in fact, risen to such dangerous proportions that the Director of National Intelligence has reportedly launched a National Intelligence Estimate to examine the implications of the U.S. decline in manufacturing for our national security.

I believe the most direct cause for concern is clear: the more that well-subsidized foreign entities are allowed to take advantage of our open market-oriented procurement policies, the greater the likelihood that our

3

Defense Department will one day find that no domestic manufacturer exists for a critical piece of material.

In other words, as our vital defense jobs and technology continue to be outsourced, I believe that our very national security is put at risk.

This is not a concern directed solely at China. The Ansonia Copper and Brass Company of Waterbury, Connecticut, again, in my district, for example, is the sole domestic producer of wide diameter copper nickel tubing, which is used by the Defense Department, but it has been detrimentally impacted by the apparent price manipulation of a European firm and is now struggling to stay afloat, with the loss of countless jobs.

Nonetheless, the practices of China's state-owned enterprises are of paramount concern to us. Their heavily-subsidized entities are decimating critical manufacturing sectors here in America such as steel and electronic equipment parts.

When it comes to aerospace, China's advancement in recent years can be attributed to government support for their aircraft manufacturers, namely, Aviation Industry Corporation of China, AVIC, and the Commercial Aircraft Corporation of China, C-O-M-A-C, COMAC, and its cooperative ventures with the world's leading aerospace firms.

In these ventures, China selects a foreign aircraft manufacturer to supply China with commercial aircraft with the condition that the supplier establish a local production facility.

China's intent is to gain technology transfers to its own manufacturing industry through such agreements while the supplier gains access to low-cost Chinese labor.

As China develops its civilian capabilities, the dual-use nature of these capabilities allows it to then develop its military capabilities, and today, with help from multinational companies, AVIC is producing civilian and military aircraft to compete in foreign markets, Including the C-919 passenger jet, which will compete with the Boeing 737.

It is developing the J-20 stealth fighter, a rival of the F-22, which conducted its first public test flight earlier this year while Secretary Gates was visiting China.

Most recently, it was reported that AVIC may team with a California-based aerospace company to offer the AC-313 helicopter, the largest developed in China to date, to bid on the new presidential helicopter program, the Marine One helicopter.

While some may consider the possibility of AVIC getting this contract remote, we need to be cognizant of the fact that others may see contracts involving Chinese firms as a way to improve ties with Beijing and to lower DOD costs at a time when cutting spending is front and center in Washington.

In response to these reports, I introduced a bipartisan resolution with my colleague Frank Wolf, and I'm proud to say that there are 21 cosponsors.

We obviously need more, but there are 12 Democrats and nine Republicans so it is truly a bipartisan piece of legislation.

It is supported by my colleague Maurice Hinchey of New York, who I understand is going to testify in front of the Commission later this morning.

This argues that the Defense Department should not consider a bid on the Marine One helicopter involving any entity controlled, directed, or influenced by China.

The resolution also states that Congress will not fund this or any other defense system if the contract award involves any entity controlled, directed or influenced by the Chinese government.

And recognizing the vital role of our aerospace industry, it urges the Defense Department to limit its procurement of the new presidential helicopter and any other system to products manufactured in the United States, primarily with U.S.-made parts.

In Stratford, Connecticut, which is in my district, we have Sikorsky Aircraft. The facility has approximately 9,000 employees manufacturing the best commercial and military helicopters in the world, including the Black Hawk and Marine One, and I am just recently back, as of last weekend, from Afghanistan where I flew in Black Hawk helicopters, and talked with military, both rank and file and the brass, about the Black Hawk and the role that it is playing today in our security and our efforts in Afghanistan.

The Marine One helicopter has been produced in Stratford, Connecticut since 1958 and the presidency of Dwight Eisenhower.

Sikorsky has been cooperating with China on helicopter developments since 1995. It is not necessarily clear that the answer to this challenge is to curtail that cooperation or the cooperation occurring with aerospace firms across the industry, including Pratt and Whitney, which is also a major employer in Connecticut, and which is, in fact, supplying the engines for the AC-313.

But it is clear that we cannot allow a Chinese state-owned enterprise to take advantage of our open procurement process to compete for military contracts, and I believe we should be wary of the implications of China's advancements on the commercial side on U.S. manufacturing as well. This trend is exemplified by AVIC's current attempt to buy Minnesota-based private-aircraft maker Cirrus Industries, their line of four-seat propeller aircraft.

When we outsource our manufacturing jobs and our technology, it severely hurts our economic and our national security.

Ladies and gentlemen, we are a nation today that consumes. We no longer build. We need to be in the building business. It is about our technology, and when we outsource the jobs, we outsource the technology-- make no mistake about that--and it goes elsewhere, and then we are continually not on the cutting edge of new technology and new development for the next generation of helicopters and anything else. We cannot rely on other countries, regardless of whether they are allies or adversaries, to supply defense-related materials.

And we certainly cannot allow Chinese companies that do not play by global trade rules to compete for these government contracts.

As I said, the damaging effects of these policies are being felt in my state right now. From the days of Eli Whitney, Connecticut has always been known as a vital center of industrial and manufacturing innovation in America, and that's how we came by the name of being the quote, "Arsenal of the Republic," and companies like Ansonia Copper and Brass, Pratt and Whitney, and Sikorsky are proud inheritors of this fine Connecticut tradition.

But right now, we are the canary in the coal mine. If these trends in defense outsourcing continue, we will not only continue to lose high-skilled defense manufacturing jobs in Connecticut and all across America, but, again, I believe that we put our national security at risk as well.

And I thank you very, very much for the opportunity to come before you this morning and ask you to heed my comments and those of others as we, yes, look at how we want to be part of a global competitive market, but let's not do it at the risk of our own economic and industrial base and the jobs that these have historically allowed for workers to become part of the middle class of this country and to be able to make their way and be economically viable for their security and the security of their families.

I thank you very, very much.

HEARING CO-CHAIR WESSEL: Thank you for appearing before us this morning.

I know your time is short, and I believe there is a comment by one Commissioner, very quick, and we'll let you get back on your busy schedule.

MS. DeLAURO: Thank you very much.

HEARING CO-CHAIR WESSEL: Appreciate your leadership on this issue.

MS. DeLAURO: Thank you.

COMMISSIONER D'AMATO: Thank you, Mr. Chairman.

Congressman DeLauro, I wanted to welcome you to the hearing and thank you very much for your testimony. I remember fondly the days when you and I were both representing Connecticut in a staff position. I was with Senator Ribicoff; you were with Senator Dodd. We did a few things together then.

I commend you for your passion on outsourcing and preserving our high-tech base and jobs, particularly for the industry in Connecticut, and I hope that your legislative initiative gets widely debated, and that we can move forward to doing some things here in the Congress that need to be done legislatively that aren't being done elsewhere, Congresswoman.

MS. DeLAURO: Thank you so very much and a proud heritage, and I have very, very fond memories of Senator Ribicoff and clearly Senator Dodd's race up to be the newly elected replacement for the Senator though Abe Ribicoff will never be replaced.

And I thank you, and it's our hope that we can in a bipartisan basis make this piece of legislation a part of our defense legislation as we move forward.

COMMISSIONER D'AMATO: Thank you. We hope so.

MS. DeLAURO: Thank you very much.

HEARING CO-CHAIR WESSEL: Thank you.

COMMISSIONER D'AMATO: Thank you.

OPENING STATEMENT OF VICE CHAIRMAN DANIEL M. SLANE
HEARING CO-CHAIR

VICE CHAIRMAN SLANE: We're going to start with the first panel if we can have our two panelists come forward.

Congressman Michaud has submitted a written statement, which we will put into the record.

And we will impose upon our two panelists to take a break in about 20 minutes when Congressman Hinchey arrives, and we'll take his statement.

Dr. Barry J. Naughton is a Professor of Chinese Economy and the Sokwanlok Chair of Chinese International Affairs at the University of California.

Dr. Naughton is an authority on the Chinese economy with an emphasis on issues relating to industry, trade, finance and China's transition to a market economy. His recent research focuses on regional economic growth in the People's Republic of China and the relationship between foreign trade and investment and regional growth. He is also completing a general textbook on the Chinese economy.

Dr. Naughton has appeared before the Commission in the past, most recently at a 2007 hearing on government control of Chinese economy.

Dr. Derek Scissors is a Research Fellow at the Heritage Foundation in Washington. Dr. Scissors focuses his studies on the economies of China and India and analyzes and comments on broader economic trends in Asia, as well as related challenges facing the United States.

Dr. Scissors is also an adjunct professor at George Washington University where he teaches a course on the Chinese economy.

Before joining Heritage in August of 2008, he was China economist at Intelligence Research, a global consulting firm.

Dr. Scissors' most recent testimony before the Commission was at last year's hearing on Chinese holding of U.S. debt.

Thank you, gentlemen, for taking the time to come, and we'll start with Dr. Scissors.

PANEL II: STATE-OWNED ENTERPRISES IN CHINA

STATEMENT OF DR. DEREK SCISSORS
RESEARCH FELLOW IN ASIA ECONOMICS,
THE HERITAGE FOUNDATION, WASHINGTON, D.C.

DR. SCISSORS: Thank you, Mr. Chairman, and the rest of the Commission, for having me back. I'm glad to be here. I'm hoping that we'll have a vigorous discussion if not of the state of Chinese state-owned enterprises, then of the U.S. policy response.

I'm going to do a little bit of history at the beginning, just because I think the history is really relevant.

This is a data situation that's a curve. If you refer back to 1980 and 1990 as the reference point, you have a completely different picture than if you refer back to the year 2000, in my opinion. So back to 1980 and 1990, the state sector looks completely different and the economy looks completely different.

If you use even 1990--so 1980 seems a little easy-reform started in 1978 formally--if you use even 1990, state-owned enterprises are very different than they were, and there are many more non-state enterprises, including genuinely private enterprises.

On the other hand, if you use 2001, for example, ten years ago, the privatization trend, in my opinion, has been reversed both in terms of changing the nature of state-owned enterprises and in terms of the mix of firms that exist in the economy.

So a lot of the debate here is if you start back 25 years ago, everything looks like it's pretty good. You start back ten years ago, in my opinion, it doesn't look so good, and I just want everyone to keep that in mind because that's going to underlay most of our possible disagreements.

I want to cite two elements that are in my written testimony that are important and they're recent. In 2006, December 2006, the State Council lays out a list of areas where the state must lead, and the Chinese translation of this is a little bit vague for our purposes, unfortunately, and the English translation is just bad, but I'll read it to you anyway.

The list of enterprises where the state must solely own or have a majority share in, and, again, this is not a good translation, are everything having to do with power, oil, petrochemicals, gas, telecom and armaments.

The state must also control--whatever that means--coal, aviation, shipping. State-owned enterprises should also be the heavyweights in machinery, autos, IT, construction, iron and steel and non-ferrous metals.

Now I'm giving you this long list, which by the way leaves out banking, insurance, the rest of finance, media, tobacco and railways, because you're going to start to wonder after awhile, well, what's left? And that is the point I want to raise to you.

In December 2006, we got a statement from the Chinese government, central government, that really most of the economy has to be reserved for state-owned enterprises in some way that they have not defined. That's one point.

And the second one was thankfully provided to me by the always reliable Wu Bangguo, who is number two in the Chinese Party hierarchy, and who at the National People's Congress a few weeks ago threw in one of the things the Party will never allow is privatization. Just in case you were wondering--

[Laughter.]

DR. SCISSORS: --that will never happen. Along with democratization and all the things that we already knew that they weren't going to allow.

So those are a few comments indicating why I think since 2001, we've seen a reversal even though since 1980, we've clearly seen tremendous progress.

The major, the pivot point in this debate, and I hope that Professor Naughton and I have significant disagreement because I think that will be useful for the Commission, the pivot--and also because I like to fight--let's be honest.

[Laughter.]

DR. SCISSORS: The pivot point for the debate in a lot of cases is the definition of "non-state." The Chinese use "non-state." That a lot of times for foreigners gets translated to private. Non-state does not mean private and China doesn't make this mistake. We're the ones who make the mistake, and I'm going to flesh that out at great length.

But you'll see people talking about the private sector having 60 percent of the economy, and they mean the non-state sector. That itself is a difficult contention to prove, but they don't mean the private sector, and they just slip into that language.

So, on one hand, we're going to get to the fact that if you're a state-owned enterprise that's very different from a state-owned enterprise 25 years ago, what should you be called? The Chinese will call you a state-owned enterprise. They'll say SOEs have to be heavyweights in these sectors, and they mean these kinds of state firms. But those state firms are completely different than they were.

So if you want to call them something different, you want to call them state-controlled instead of state-owned, okay. But the Chinese refer to them as state-owned and, as they say, the state most dominate oil, it must dominate iron ore, et cetera.

Firms like Sinopec, China Mobile, the big firms that we recognize around the world as having a global position, they have a shareholding structure. They have listed subsidiaries that are very large that have shares owned by retail investors, individuals, private firms, and so on. Beijing calls them "state firms." They are required to control key sectors, and the key sectors have to be controlled by the state.

So there's a terminological problem. There's an obvious one, which is non-state doesn't equal private, and people shouldn't act as if it does, and then there's a complicated one involving what do we call these state firms?

And I want to throw some numbers at you. They're in my written statement. But the private sector, what China calls the private sector, constituted 11 percent of domestic investment--sorry--of total investment in 2004 and 21 percent in 2010. That's a big increase. So if you want to say the private sector is waxing in China, you have evidence. It went from 11 percent of investment in 2004 to 21 percent in 2010.

On the other hand, the private sector is 21 percent of investment in 2010. It's not 60 percent, it's not 70 percent, it's 20 percent. What else is going on here is that, that what China calls the "state sector" is around 40 percent through this period, and what they call "limited liability corporations" jump up to about 24 percent, and the foreign share declines. And foreign share declining is one of the main things you guys talk about over the years.

The 24 percent for limited liability corporations tends to be what we're focused on here. If you put that 24 percent in with the state sector, the explicit state sector, you get the state controlling over 60 percent of investment, which in my opinion is the accurate number.

If you want to say, hey, this is broken out differently by the Chinese, a limited liability corporation sounds like the private sector to me, and put it over in the private sector, you get the private sector at 45 percent of the economy.

Why do I think these limited liability corporations are state-owned? First of all, there's a category, there are two categories in the Chinese official breakdown. One says wholly state- owned, and one says non-wholly state-owned. This is a little bit of a hint for me.

The other thing is that a lot of the limited liability corporations are, in fact, the state giants that we recognize as dominant state firms, like CNPC which has a listed subsidiary of PetroChina.

So we don't know that all limited liability corporations are state-owned. We know that the biggest ones, it is natural and obvious to regard them as state-owned, and we also know that the Chinese divide them up in such a way that it implies they think a lot of them are state-controlled.

So I can't give you this definitive answer that all limited liability corporations are state-owned, the state controls 62 percent of investment exactly, but the case for saying the private sector is 60 to 70 percent of the economy is extremely weak.

The case for saying the non-state sector is 60 to 70 percent of the economy is better, but it's still subject to this qualification of what would we really call these non-state firms if we had really good information about them? I tend to call the largest ones state-owned. Perhaps Professor Naughton disagrees.

There are a lot of other numbers I can throw at you about shares of trade and so on, but we would like to keep the testimony brief so I'm just going to jump to the political implications.

One of the things that is now just being realized is these state, these giant state firms, it's not just that the Party tells the state firms what to do. That used to be the case. It is no longer just that. Of course, the Party has tremendous influence over state firms, but you're now seeing state firms pushing back:

You set us up as national champions. We represent China globally. We provide tons of tax revenue. We provide tons of employment. We're China's representatives overseas. Don't make policies that hurt us.

So we have the beginnings of two-way influence between a state sector and the Party and the central government that is going to make it harder for China to unwind this what I see as a ten-year trend moving back in the direction of the state.

And you've seen that. The State Council started in 2004. Premier Wen started in about 2006 saying, hey, we overinvest; we need to move towards a rebalance, more consumption-oriented economy, and China has completely failed to do so.

And there's a specific political economy reason: they got really big firms; the state sector has been exalted by this investment. It's inefficient. It needs more capital inputs than the private sector. Investment is a natural way to prop up state firms, and if you take that investment away, they shrink, and they don't like it.

So we have a specific reason why China has failed to rebalance. You all are familiar with specific reasons why the United States has failed to rebalance. Chinese reason is not that different.

I'll close by saying this makes for a really big political challenge for the U.S. I don't want to take us off track, but in my opinion, the status of state-owned enterprises is far more important in U.S. economic policymaking than the pegged currency, and it's going to be very, very difficult to get the Chinese to change.

They are wedded to it economically. They're to some extent wedded to it politically. We have factions in China that are on our side, but there are very powerful factions arrayed against the kind of reform that the U.S. really needs to improve the bilateral relationship. I think that's a challenge for the Commission and for broader U.S. policy going forward.

Thank you.

[The written statement follows:]

PREPARED STATEMENT OF DEREK SCISSORS, RESEARCH FELLOW IN ASIA ECONOMICS THE HERITAGE FOUNDATION

There are two basic observations concerning state-owned enterprises in China:

(i) The large majority operate very differently than they did 20 or even 15 years ago, and
(ii) They account for far more of the economy than popularly believed.

These observations serve to reconcile debates over the state sector. It is certainly true that there has been an important and considerable change in the Chinese economy as a result of changes in state-owned enterprises (SOEs). However, it is not true that SOEs have faded into the background or that they are no longer "state-owned enterprises." In fact, the state sector and non-market behavior still predominate on most measures.

History Sketch

Phase 1 (1979-1986): SOEs, broadly understood, are allowed to move beyond the plan
Phase 2 (1987-1992): Partly commercial entities arise
Phase 3 (1993-2001): The state sector shrinks; the truly private sector expands
Phase 4 (2002-2007): Restructuring of SOEs; contraction ends
Phase 5: (2008-present) Active re-enlargement of state sector
Phase 6: (2014?): SOEs exert greater political influence

Disputes over the historical progression of SOEs are unavoidable, but it is clear much has changed. There were no true commercial entities in the PRC in 1975, because there were no markets in which to operate. In the latter half of the 1970s, agricultural cooperatives (effectively rural SOEs) in certain counties were permitted to act independently if they first met planned economy requirements. This independence was formalized at the fall 1978 Communist Party plenum, signifying the start of the reform period.

By the mid-1980s, quasi-state entities began appearing. These included town and village enterprises and firms with minority foreign ownership. These were technically controlled by the state but they had commercial latitude. In some ways, they were the forerunner of current SOEs. This type of firm grew in number and importance for more than a decade.

For much of the 1990s, many SOEs were partly or entirely sold. They were replaced in some cases by quasi-state enterprises which looked much like the old SOEs utilizing some commercial operating principles. However, they were replaced in other cases by private firms, including foreign majority-controlled companies and the first domestic genuinely private firms with more than just a few employees.[1]

The sale of public assets was slowed by economic duress from the Asian financial crisis and political criticism in the late 1990s. Shrinking the state sector was replaced by "reform." This reform has been widely misconstrued. It consisted of converting most SOEs into share-holding entities, which had explicit state entities as majority holders but also sold stock in Shanghai, Hong Kong, or elsewhere. These share-holding firms took on multiple characteristics of truly commercial operations, including some form of profit orientation and public reporting, but they were still state-controlled and directed.[2]

At some (disputable) point in the mid-2000s, the reform process was reversed entirely and SOEs began to wax again. The reversal can reasonable be dated to late 2006, when the State Council formally set aside the core of the economy for SOEs,[3]

---

[1] Yasheng Huang, *Capitalism with Chinese Characteristics: Entrepreneurship and the State* (Cambridge: Cambridge University Press, 2008).
[2] OECD, "China: Defining the Boundary Between the Market and the State," 2009, at
http://www.oecd.org/dataoecd/35/45/42390089.pdf
3 Zhao Huanxin, "China names key industries for absolute state control," *China Daily*, December 19, 2006, at

[T]he State should solely own, or have a majority share in, enterprises engaged in power generation and distribution, oil, petrochemicals and natural gas, telecom and armaments. The State must also have a controlling stake in the coal, aviation, and shipping industries.... Central SOEs should also become heavyweights in sectors including machinery, automobiles, IT, construction, iron and steel, and non-ferrous metals.

This omits state dominance in banking, insurance, and the rest of finance, media, tobacco, and railways. This was a daunting list, representing a wide swath of the economy set apart for state distortions. The reversal was codified by Wu Bangguo, second in the Party hierarchy, when he listed privatization with other intolerable developments.[4]

We have made a solemn declaration that we will not employ a system of multiple parties holding office in rotation; diversify our guiding thought; separate executive, legislative and judicial powers; use a bicameral or federal system; or *carry out privatization* (emphasis added)

SOE Features

The discussion of SOEs has been undermined by a fundamental error: the conflation of restructured, share-holding firms with the truly private sector. Share-holding SOEs are manifestly not private actors and assessments of the corporate sector that assume so are fatally flawed from the outset. The origin of this mistake is historical. As quasi-state entities emerged and proliferated, it was clear some sort of separate treatment was necessary and the concept of "non-state" was created. This was never intended to indicate "private"—quite the opposite: it was meant to signify that the creation of corporate forms quite different from SOEs could occur without privatization and its ideological pitfalls.

The meaning of "non-state" is very well understood by the Chinese government. The (sometimes willful) misunderstanding outside China rests on two shaky pillars. The first is a mis-rendering of "non-state"—where the PRC sees the opposite of state as non-state, many foreign observers see the opposite of state as "private" and simply re-label accordingly. The second is more sophisticated and based on the share-holding change.

Neither specification of share-holders nor sale of stock by itself does anything to alter state control. The large majority of firms listed on domestic stock markets are specifically designated as state-owned.[5] The sale of small minority stakes on foreign exchanges could be construed as recasting mainstays such as CNPC (through its list vehicle PetroChina), China Mobile, and Chinalco as non-state entities of some form. However, they are still centrally directed SOEs, as explicitly indicated by the Chinese government.

More broadly, firms are defined by inputs and outputs. Most Chinese firms sell in a market environment that is unrecognizably different from the operating environment in 1975 and sharply different even from the one in 1995. In this sense almost none of them are still traditional Chinese SOEs. On the output side, however, the requirement that the state predominate in so many sectors is meant to sharply confine competition, so that SOEs operate within markets but they operate primarily within state-controlled markets. This regulatory protection is the most powerful subsidy many SOEs receive.

The input side also continues to distinguish SOEs clearly from foreign or domestic private companies. Production inputs comprise labor, capital, land, and other physical resources such as energy. For SOEs, including those which

---

http://www.chinadaily.com.cn/china/2006-12/19/content_762056.htm

[4] Michael Sainsbury, "China Rules Out Political Reform," *The Australian*, March 14, 2011, at http://www.theaustralian.com.au/news/world/china-rules-out-political-reform/story-e6frg6so-1226020720813

[5] Vincent Fernanado, "Here's Why Chinese Stocks Remain a State-Controlled Façade," Business Insider, June 22, 2010, at http://www.businessinsider.com/heres-why-chinese-stocks-are-a-state-controlled-facade-2010-6

have completed share-holding reform, all of these show the state's overwhelming role. It is routine for Chinese officials to bounce back and forth from corporate to government posts at the behest of the Party, no less so at China Mobile and the like than anywhere else.[6]

In stark contrast to private firms, which often cannot buy land at any price, SOEs have immediate call on free land, which is all technically owned by the state. The main barrier to SOEs acquiring land is other SOEs. SOEs as a matter of course also receive hefty power and other input subsidies not available to genuinely private firms

As for capital, every aspect is dominated by the state. All large financial institutions are state-owned, the People's Bank assigns loan quotas every year, and, within these quotas, lending is directed according to state priorities. Interest rates are also controlled, and last year real borrowing costs were barely above zero. Conveniently, then, loan quotas and bank practices strongly inhibit non-state borrowing. Securities markets are also dominated by the state. As an illustration, the volume of government bond issuance utterly dwarfs corporate bonds and is growing relentlessly, crowding out private firms.

SOE Investment Share

The popular question regarding SOEs is what portion of the economy do they comprise? The one clear answer is: significantly smaller than the 100 percent share 35 years ago, as well as smaller than the somewhat uncertain share 20 years ago.

Beyond that, the State Statistical Bureau (SSB) provides insufficiently precise data. Even the number of SOEs is not published. There are fewer than 120 centrally controlled SOEs, and the number is still slowly shrinking. These, however, typically each have dozens of subsidiaries, including nearly all the Chinese companies most people are familiar with. There are also thousands of provincially and municipally controlled SOEs. Meanwhile, truly private firms number in the tens of millions, though are comparatively very small. There are also millions of firms of mixed or unclear status.

Data provision for urban fixed investment was considerably enhanced starting in 2004. For the PRC, urban fixed investment is critical, because it drives the economy. In 2004, urban investment stood at 5.9 trillion yuan and was equivalent to 43 percent of GDP. Just six years later, it was a stunning 24.1 trillion yuan and equivalent to 61 percent of GDP.[7] The Chinese economy was formerly driven by exports; it is now driven by urban investment (2010 rural investment was only 3.7 trillion yuan).

Table 1: Urban Investment Shares (percent)

	State-owned	Limited liability Corp.	Domestic private	Wholly foreign-owned	Partly foreign-owned	Share-holding	Other mixed ownership
2004	44.0	20.8	11.1	4.5	7.3	9.3	3.0
2007	36.9	23.6	18.3	5.2	5.2	7.8	3.1
2010	38.0	24.3	21.1	3.3	3.3	6.7	3.4

Because urban investment has almost quadrupled, all raw figures have increased and even the clearly waning foreign role represents greater absolute investment. Volume comparisons over time are thus misleading. An

---

[6] Chen Jialu, "CEO Reshuffles Signal New View of Watchdog," *China Daily*, August 24, 2010, at
http://www.chinadaily.com.cn/bizchina/2010-08/24/content_11194717.htm
[7] All figures in this section, including the table, are taken from China Monthly Statistics, Volume 12, 2004 – Volume 1, 2011, National Bureau of Statistics, Beijing.

unmistakable trend is dynamic growth in what the SSB labels as private investment. Domestic private investment may have been undercounted in 2004 but, regardless, it is now in excess of one-fifth of total investment.

Against that, what the SSB labels as the state-owned share is not quite two-fifths. This figure corroborates claims that the non-state sector comprises 60 percent or more of the economy. But it hardly indicates the private sector is anything like that large—with wholly owned foreign investment, the genuinely private share is a bit short of 25 percent. The other 38 percent often called "private" is of various kinds of mixed ownership.

Within this mixed grouping, there are three lesser categories. To qualify as partly foreign owned, a firm need be only 25 percent foreign-invested, even if the majority partner is state or private. Yet this figure is still small and declining. Shareholding is larger but also declining. "Other" ownership is small. The bulk of the mixed ownership category is limited liability corporations (LLC), which are approximately equal in share to what is officially designated as the private—domestic plus foreign—sector.

What is this last group? It is manifestly not private. It has always been treated separately from domestic private companies. It includes subsidiaries of centrally controlled state giants such as Sinochem. Most important, it necessarily overlaps greatly with sectors that are required or admitted to be dominated by the state. The best single characterization of this group is that it is organized and behaves in a way that is starkly different than the SOEs of 1990, but that the bulk of LLC investment is still controlled by the state.

In sum, the verifiable private sector accounts for one-fourth of urban investment. That share has risen since 2004, though the rate of climb has more recently slowed.

Other Measurements

Beyond investment, information is scattered. Chinese industrial production data are often used to represent GDP and then to divine state and private shares of the economy. This is a mistake for several reasons, the most immediate being that the production data do not even accurately portray production. They have always been internally inconsistent and, starting in 2006, were split into categories seemingly chosen to obfuscate.

The best guess is that the truly private share of industrial production is somewhat higher than it is for investment. As private firms are universally accepted— even by the Chinese government—to be more efficient than SOEs, their share of inputs such as investment and employment will be higher than their share of outputs such as production or sales. A reasonable range for the genuinely private share of production is thus 30-35 percent.

Elsewhere, reporting by SOEs is notoriously bad. However, it is suggestive, at least, that China National Petroleum and China Mobile claim more 2009 profits than the top 500 firms combined. The State-owned Assets Supervision and Administration Commission indicates that the assets of its firms have grown from the equivalent of 60 percent of GDP in mid-2003 to 62 percent of GDP in mid-2010, despite the rapid GDP gains during that period.[8]

Official data on employment are again limited to cities but not as detailed as for investment. Through the third quarter of 2010, the explicit state share of employment was 57 percent, though that is well below the 74 percent announced seven years earlier. Unfortunately, the non-state share is here designated only as "other," which obscures whether this includes restructured firms that are still manifestly state-controlled, as in the investment categories. The sectors which SOEs must or plainly do dominate accounted for 80 percent of the capitalization of domestic stock exchanges at the end of 2010. Similarly, tax revenue from private domestic firms is less than 15

---

[8] Zhou Xin and Simon Rabinovitch, "China Inc Gets New Chairman as State-Owned Firms' Clout Grows," Reuters, September 6, 2010, at http://uk.reuters.com/article/2010/09/06/business-us-china-economy-state-idUKTRE68514720100906 and "China state giants outstrip private firms," Channel News Asia, August 30, 2010, at http://www.channelnewsasia.com/stories/afp_asiapacific_business/view/1077996/1/.html

percent of the total.[9]

Trade is an area of private sector strength. Domestic private firms generated 30 percent of exports in 2010. In addition, foreign-funded enterprises account for over half of total trade.[10] However, since "foreign-funded" can still include a private or state majority owner, these numbers cannot simply be added. Still, the combined private share of trade is considerably higher than it is in investment and may exceed 40 percent of volume.

In contrast, SOEs utterly dominate outward investment. The Heritage Foundation's China Global Investment Tracker provides information on the size and originating company, among other aspects, for large Chinese non-bond investments since the start of 2005.[11] It corresponds well to official figures but contains far more information.

On Heritage data, total non-state investment appears to be below $13 billion since 2005, which is less than 6 percent of the total. The four largest investors—China National Petroleum, China National Petrochemical, China Investment Corp. (CIC), and China Aluminum—alone accounted for half of Chinese investment through the end of 2010. All are centrally controlled, with CIC one of the two sovereign funds.

All large investors, such as such as China Minmetals and Industrial and Commercial Bank of China, are centrally controlled. This reflects the national champion concept, that the PRC should have national firms with economies of scale sufficient to be competitive on global markets. Almost all firms that might qualify as national champions are SOEs.

Can SOEs Be Rolled Back?

A distinct policy related to the status of SOEs is consolidation—shrinking the number of firms in an industry to curb "disorderly competition." Industries range from autos to yarn.[12] Where market concentration is high, the State Development and Reform Commission preserves it. For example, to avoid competition cutting into crude oil profits and driving out inefficient suppliers, it hiked taxes for crude on the state giants but subsidized them in refining where they face competitors.[13] This ensured state involvement at all points, so the suppression of competition fit perfectly with the all-too-visible hand.

The suppression of competition coincident with regulatory protection of SOEs combine to guarantee SOEs will have relatively more weight. Optimists correctly point out that SOEs shrank in importance for most of the reform period and current pro-state policies can be reversed (again). That is certainly true, but may be quite difficult.

---

[9] China Monthly Statistics Volume 1, 2011 National Bureau of Statistics Beijing and "China Stimulus Plan Criticized for 'Crowding Out' Private Sector," China Stakes, August 7, 2009, at http://www.chinastakes.com/2009/8/china-stimulus-plan-criticized-for-crowding-out-private-sector.html

[10] Wang Xiaotian, "Private Enterprise Exports Skyrocket," *China Daily*, February 9, 2011, at http://www.chinadaily.com.cn/business/2011-02/09/content_11967514.htm and Ministry of Commerce, People's Republic of China, "China's Absorption of FDI," July 21, 2010, at http://english.mofcom.gov.cn/aarticle/statistic/foreigninvestment/201008/20100807086430.html

[11] Derek Scissors, "China Global Investment Tracker: 2011," The Heritage Foundation, January 10, 2011, at *http://www.heritage.org/research/reports/2011/01/china-global-investment-tracker-2011*.

[12] "Measures to Stop Disorderly Competition," People's Daily Online, March 2, 2005, at http://english.peopledaily.com.cn/200503/02/eng20050302_175221.html and Vivian Wai-yin Kwok, "Beijing Redeploys Its Carmakers For Global Race," Forbes.com, March 23, 2009, at http://www.forbes.com/2009/03/23/china-auto-stimulus-markets-equity-consolidation.html

[13] Zhu Qiwen, "Time to Take a Fresh Look at Oil Subsidies," *China Daily*, March 21, 2008, at http://www.chinadaily.com.cn/opinion/2008-03/21/content_6554797.htm

The national champions concept began to be discussed in the PRC in the late 1990s. At that time, there was no question about the hierarchy involved: the government would consider creating national champions and SOEs so blessed would remain entirely subservient, as they had for the previous fifty years. That hierarchy is no longer so clear.

Some SOEs are now truly gigantic, not just on a national scale but a global one. The steel industry is grotesquely oversized in the international economy. National banks are on some measures the world's largest, as are Chinese telecoms.[14] The oil majors provide large chunks of national tax revenue. And State Grid dwarfs them all. They are the PRC's global representatives, provide the government with much of its money and, more important, generate massive and steady employment. They are also run by high-level Party cadres or, in some cases, their children. When the next economic reformer takes the reins as Premier and pushes the SOEs, they will push back powerfully.

The situation presents a severe challenge to the U.S. In most sectors, there is no market of 1.3 billion. Instead, there is what is left after the SOEs are handed the bulk. This applies, of course, to American companies looking to serve the Chinese market. It is no surprise that official data indicate the foreign investment share has plummeted in the past few years. The truncated market extends to U.S. exports. The various forms of subsidy provided to SOEs are far bigger barriers to American goods than the yuan's peg to the dollar. Subsidization has been and can be increased to offset currency changes.

More generally, massive bilateral economic imbalances are on the Chinese side caused by overinvestment and underconsumption. The PRC overinvests precisely to enable SOEs to retain dominant positions despite their inefficiency. To sustain this overinvestment, consumption must effectively be taxed. The regulatory suppression of competition discourages consumers and generates additional profit to finance SOE investment. Capital subsidies also finance investment and, though the state-run banking system, transfer income from households to SOEs via controlled interest rates.

In the new five-year plan, the PRC is once again touting rebalancing. It has done so since 2004 and matters have only worsened. There is a very good reason for this: rebalancing would undermine SOEs, when the thrust of policy is to exalt them. For China to actually rebalance, Beijing will have to accept a retrenchment of SOEs and this process will be stridently opposed. It is strongly in America's interest to assist, by reorienting bilateral economic policy toward making retrenchment of SOEs by various means the top goal.

VICE CHAIRMAN SLANE: Dr. Naughton.

STATEMENT OF DR. BARRY J. NAUGHTON
ROFESSOR OF CHINESE ECONOMY, UNIVERSITY OF
CALIFORNIA, SAN DIEGO, LA JOLLA, CALIFORNIA

DR. NAUGHTON: I don't think we're going to get as vigorous a debate as you would like. I find I agree with almost everything that Derek Scissors said.

Obviously, I would give slightly different emphasis to certain aspects

---

[14] Philip Lagerkranser, "China Banks Surge to World's Largest May Be Too Good to Be True," Bloomberg.com, April 29, 2009, at http://www.bloomberg.com/apps/news?pid=newsarchive&sid=aueh06DOY37A and Janet Ong, "China Tells Telecom Companies to Merge in Overhaul (Update 1), Bloomberg.com, May 25, 2008, at http://www.bloomberg.com/apps/news?pid=newsarchive&sid=aYQg0d5NANkM

of the story, but overall the story that I would tell would be, I think, quite similar.

We are looking at a China where we saw dramatic progress in the destatization of the economy up through about 2003. Actually when I had the honor of testifying before this Committee in 2007, I said, at that point: look, one of the main things we see is a stabilization of state ownership, its concentration in certain key sectors, continued efforts at reform going along with the stabilization of the state sector, and at that point laying out ambitious new development priorities in the 11th Five Year Plan and the Medium and Long-Term Plan for Technology Development.

But it was too early at that point to really see whether those initiatives were serious and whether they were going to come to something because from that point, looking backwards, most of the previous Chinese plans hadn't amounted to a whole lot.

Four years later, what we see is that these same observations, I think, are still the key trends that we should use to structure how we look at the Chinese state sector, but the trends are worse in every one of these dimensions.

So, for instance, if we look at stabilization of central government state sector, again, as Derek said, now it's not just stabilization; it's also a political reassertion of the fundamental importance of these state-owned firms that we didn't see five years ago.

Five years ago was a sort of a pragmatic compromise: well, what are we going to do with natural resource sectors? We're worried about foreigners coming in; we're not so comfortable with private firms doing it. Maybe we'll hold on to it for the state. But now it's become something much, much more explicit.

The central government state-owned sector has been growing. If we take the primarily industrial firms under SASAC, which is the key central government body that manages these firms, it had about 8.6 million employees in 2002, and 12 million at the end of 2009.

So these are big firms, and they're getting bigger. If we looked at their capital, at their value, the increase would be, of course, much greater because they're more profitable and they're growing.

When we look at the state sector overall, those increases are actually almost exactly balanced out by reductions in state sector employment in smaller scale, more competitive, previously locally-run sectors.

So the state sector, as a whole, isn't getting bigger, but the companies that we care about, that have a big global impact and have big influence, they're getting bigger, and of course, as the Chinese economy is getting bigger, they're obviously playing a more important global role.

Number two, the reform impulse. When we say that the large state firms were stabilized, of course, part of that stabilization was trying to make them into more efficient corporations, repackaging them, giving them modern corporate governance structures and to a certain extent listing them on the public stock markets in China.

That process, that impulse, the reform impulse, has clearly weakened over the last five years. Li Rongrong who was the first head of SASAC had a very ambitious agenda to reorganize and shrink down all these companies to less than a hundred large-scale competitive firms, and also to take each one of these and reorganize them into an integral corporation so it didn't have any sort of bureaucratic elements, it wouldn't have any loss-making, hidden slush funds and all this stuff, and he failed. He failed in both those efforts.

The number of companies did not shrink down to under a hundred, and the number of those companies that have been reorganized integrally into modern joint stock corporations in this way, they claim 20, but that's a stretch at best.

Derek referred to the effort to define sectors where the state plays a role, and he ended up concluding most of the economy is reserved for state enterprises. I don't quite agree with that interpretation, but I very much agree with him that that was a very important episode.

Essentially what it was, was a botched episode where SASAC tried to lay out a rationale for whether or not they would have state enterprises in certain sectors--natural resources, telecom, et cetera--but then they collapsed into this argument about, well, wait a minute, what about a state steel mill? There's not really justification for state ownership in the steel industry, but we do have this one really good steel mill so maybe we should allow that.

Actually what happened is that the document Derek is referring to never was published. It was supposed to be published, it was supposed to be ratified by the State Council and published, but never was. So clearly there was either some kind of political argument or some kind of decision perhaps to keep it secret, which is also possible.

The one positive thing we see in this respect is that over the last three years, the government has started collecting dividends from state firms, initially five percent, later ten percent, and more from some of the natural resource firms, which are most profitable.

So at least that does a little bit to balance off some of these concentrations of economic power, which I very much agree with Derek are shaping and distorting the whole policy process in China.

In fact, we should say quickly that part of the debate about reform in China--and reform is not going very well in China, but at least there continue to be vigorous debates--that some of the debates that get interpreted as being about democratization in the U.S. are perhaps more accurately about these concentrations of power in some of the state-owned enterprise roles. We can talk about that later if you're interested.

Finally, one last set of points, and that is along with this embrace of the state sector, we also see a much greater willingness on the part of the government to use these state-owned firms as instruments of government policy.

For example, during the stimulus program after the global financial crisis hit, state-owned enterprises boosted their investment from 20 percent of GDP to 25 percent of GDP (in 2009). Huge. And that's in state-controlled firms. So that's a massive amount of resources flowing through the state-owned firms.

We see the government much more willing to use state-owned firms as an instrument of technology development. We saw it with the telecom firms being essentially coerced into adopting the Chinese indigenous technology standard, TD-SCDMA. We see it in large engineering, so-called "mega-projects," including the large civilian airliner that the Congresswoman was talking about. We see it even in things like corporate social responsibility. This year, SASAC's big emphasis is not on reforming these big firms, but in making them into large, externally-oriented national champions. So it's clear that the focus has shifted.

So final words, the momentum is clearly there for a larger, more intrusive government role exercised through state-owned enterprises, and I think it is indeed a big challenge for us.

Thank you.

PANEL II: DISCUSSION, QUESTIONS AND ANSWERS

VICE CHAIRMAN SLANE: Thank you, Dr. Naughton.

We'll go to some questions, and I'll start with my co-chairman here, Mr. Wessel.

HEARING CO-CHAIR WESSEL: Thank you, gentlemen. Thank you both for return visits to the Commission. It's always a pleasure to have you before us.

I'd like to understand from a fairly high altitude what this means in terms of competitive pressures. From what you both described, it appears to me that the U.S. and other countries are continuing on a path towards WTO liberalization, meaning we are continuing to abide by all of our commitments that were made, tariff reductions, et cetera, and access.

And China, rather than moving towards a market economy or an economy with greater market stimuluses, if you will, is actually going in the wrong direction. You both described the fact that the sector is probably cementing itself as well as creating a more outward approach that's going to create markets overseas, brands, et cetera, et cetera, so that we're going to see much greater competitiveness in terms of their international efforts.

We have limited resources here in terms of the tools that are available. Two or three weeks ago, the WTO made a decision that limits the ability of the U.S. to respond on countervailing duties, to respond to the subsidies that are inherent in many of these state-owned enterprises, and, in 2016, the U.S. loses the automatic right to treat China as a non-market economy. It shifts to a different test.

How should we be looking at this from a competitive posture? You've described the growth of the state, but what does it mean to the U.S. in terms of how our companies compete, and what will happen with employment and other issues here?

Dr. Scissors, do you want to start?

DR. SCISSORS: Sure. It's my job here to bring a little bit of Heritage Foundation ideology to all these meetings so I'm going to start right at the beginning and get that out of the way. This isn't going to work. It's not going to work.

The Chinese have chosen to subsidize and warp their economy to subsidize bad firms in a lot of cases, not all of them. Some of them are better than others. They're not all exactly the same.

HEARING CO-CHAIR WESSEL: When you say "it's not going to work," do you mean for the Chinese or for--

DR. SCISSORS: It's not going to work for the Chinese.

HEARING CO-CHAIR WESSEL: Okay.

DR. SCISSORS: So at the aggregate level, this is not something the United States needs to worry about. The Chinese are going to waste their resources. They're doing it already, the total unnecessary environmental depletion, drop in return on capital. All of this is going to come out as their labor force switches in the middle of the decade, but, that's only one answer to your question.

So one of my answers to your question is, hey, if I'm an American policymaker looking at the long-term, I'm not worried about this. The Chinese are shooting themselves in the foot.

Now, if I'm an American businessman or somebody concerned about the short term, the picture is quite different because subsidies tend to hurt somebody. They help somebody and they hurt somebody. They hurt the people who have to pay for them and the people who have to compete against them.

I think, as a practical matter, just going down the subsidy road in the U.S., which I realize was now what you were asking, is not a good idea. We will never be able to compete with the Chinese on subsidies. They can mobilize resources far more than we can. That's the whole point of this panel, is that the Chinese have/the government has ties to these firms that the U.S. government thankfully doesn't have ties to.

Where we go, I think, first, is go after the regulatory protection. To me, the biggest subsidy is not the money that's spent. And that's why I led with a State Council statement and why Professor Naughton correctly emphasized it even though we disagree a little bit on its importance. If really huge parts of the Chinese market are reserved to these firms, if they're regional monopolies or even subsector monopolies where all of this kind of petrochemical is only produced by one company, there are economies of scales, there are monopoly profits that are available to them.

It obviously blocks American exports more fundamentally than any currency valuation you can, just as, sorry, this part of the market is not available to you.

We need to go after them on that basis. And that's not a subsidy battle. I'm not a lawyer--it is something we haven't done in the WTO, certainly something we haven't done in our bilateral negotiations. That is not going to solve all our short-term problems. In the long-term, I don't think we have a problem. But that's where I would start. The regulatory protection of these firms gives them a gigantic advantage from which everything else stems.

HEARING CO-CHAIR WESSEL: Dr. Naughton, before you start, we have Congressman Hinchey.

Just a quick comment, Dr. Scissors, which is they may be shooting themselves in the foot. My fear is they have their foot on our chest.

[Laughter.]

VICE CHAIRMAN SLANE: Thanks.

Congressman, please come up and join us. We're happy to take your statement.

HEARING CO-CHAIR WESSEL: Dr. Naughton, we'll continue with your response after Congressman Hinchey.

[CONTINUATON OF PANEL I: CONGRESSIONAL PERSPECTIVES]

VICE CHAIRMAN SLANE: Congressman Maurice Hinchey represents New York's 22nd Congressional District and sits on the House Committee on Appropriations, including the Subcommittee on Defense. He is a strong supporter of the presidential helicopter program, and in February, the Congressman sent a letter to Secretary Gates urging the Department of Defense to reject a potential bid for the presidential helicopter program from China's state-run China Aviation Industry Corporation.

The Congressman is also a cosponsor of H.R. 106, a bipartisan resolution expressing the House of Representatives' sense that the new presidential helicopter fleet should be built using products manufactured in America, and that the Defense Department should prohibit any defense acquisition bid involving any entity controlled, directed or influenced by the government of China.

Congressman, we're happy to have you with us today and look forward to your testimony.

STATEMENT OF MAURICE HINCHEY
A U.S. REPRESENTATIVE FROM THE STATE OF NEW YORK

MR. HINCHEY: Thank you very much.

It's a great pleasure for me to be here, and I deeply appreciate the attention that you're paying to this as you pay to so many things that are critically important for our country.

So I would like to start off by thanking the members and staff of the U.S.-China Economic and Security Review Commission for years of dedicated service to the Congress and the country.

Your work investigating and reporting on our relationship with China is of the utmost importance, and my colleagues and I deeply appreciate your efforts and all the recommendations that you put forward. I'm honored to have the opportunity to testify before you today and look forward to continuing to work with you if that suits you appropriately.

I will begin by saying that the United States, including our people in government, does not harbor negative wishes for China. Oftentimes, cynical, but popular, viewpoints and sound bites on China are overrepresented by a number of people--opinion makers, the press, various ways. We want the Chinese people to be successful and prosperous. We want them to be our partners in the global economy.

The United States respects the determination of the Chinese people to thrive, and the fact of the matter is that the economic fate of our two nations are very much linked together, more and more so now.

Competition serves both countries by strengthening our best business and ideas, but in order to ensure the benefits and sacrifices of the global economy, that those economies are shared, that competition must be fair.

Unfortunately, there have been unfair and unwise policies here in our own country and in China that have driven manufacturing jobs out of the United States, and a lot of those that have been driven out of the United States have gone over to China.

Far too often it seems that our major export to China is our jobs. Between 2001 and 2008, our growing trade deficit with China has cost or displaced 2.4 million jobs here from the United States. So I'd like to highlight this challenge through the renewable energy sector, which is an area that has been of special interest to me over the years, and I know it has been of great interest to you as well.

On renewable subsidies, as some of the board members may know, the solar industry has had a positive economic impact on upstate New York, in particular in the district that I represent.

Over a dozen new solar and solar-related companies have opened in the last three years, and doing so, creating hundreds of new jobs with additional jobs expected over the course of the next two years as well.

These new companies and jobs have been welcomed in a region that was severely impacted when major manufacturers shipped jobs overseas as the result of unfair free trade agreements which I strongly opposed, and I know that a lot of us have strongly opposed it.

Clean energy represents one of the most significant growth opportunities for the United States economy in decades. Businesses are starting up and thousands of new jobs are being created. At the same time, we are reducing our reliance on foreign sources of energy and protecting our environment.

Unfortunately, China is illegally subsidizing and protecting its clean energy industry at the expense of United States companies, who are being forced to compete on an uneven playing field.

This type of anti-competitive illegal activity has hurt the district that I represent, as well as towns, cities and states all across this country.

Last September, I wrote to President Obama urging him to enforce the World Trade Organization's rules for trade between nations and to ensure that China stops providing illegal subsidies for the Chinese renewable energy sector.

I'm very pleased that the administration responded to my letter and other calls for fair trade practices by launching an investigation into China's subsidies and other practices. We need to aggressively work to enforce international trade agreements to ensure a fair playing field for American businesses.

At the same time, if we want domestic industry to compete with Chinese state-owned and other Chinese companies, we need long-term strategic investments in our own renewable energy economy.

In my view, one of those investments should be made by the Department of Defense in order to promote growth in our domestic energy.

As you may know, the Department of Defense must abide by the Buy American Act when purchasing products within the department. Instead of having direct procurement, the agency has increasingly begun to rely on financing vehicles, such as Power Purchase Agreements, to fund renewable energy investments. These Power Purchase Agreements, PPAs, are attractive because they require no up-front capital costs.

Instead, a private entity installs, owns and operates a system on a military installation and sells the power to the base.

But the Buy American Act does not apply to this type of contract mechanisms. And in cases of solar energy products, there exists a de facto loophole for highly-subsidized Chinese and other foreign solar panel manufacturers to get their panels installed on military installations across the United States and across our activities in other places, allowing American solar jobs to be pushed overseas.

Some of the largest solar projects within the military rely heavily on foreign-manufactured renewable energy, including solar arrays, for example, at Nellis Air Force Base and Camp Pendleton.

To address this growing concern, I obtained language in the Fiscal Year 2011 National Defense Authorization Act to extend the Buy American Act to Power Purchase Agreements and other indirect contracts used to install our solar panels on defense facilities.

The intent of this language is to ensure the Buy American Act is applied in all cases where solar panels are installed on Department of Defense property.

So I will be working with this Congress to expand the language to other energy technologies that the Department of Defense purchases to further drive the message home that renewable energy purchasing decisions have a direct impact on the success of our nation's renewable energy manufacturing economy and our national security.

And I know how sensitive you are to all of that and how deeply understanding you are about this situation and the progress that we really have to make.

On the presidential helicopter--and I thank you very much for mentioning that just a few minutes ago--lastly, I would like to highlight the possibility that a Chinese state-owned company may manufacture the next presidential helicopter. I certainly hope that's not the case, but there is a possibility that it may happen.

I am fortunate to be working against that possibility with my friends and colleagues, including Congresswoman Rosa DeLauro, who I believe already touched here this morning.

The Wall Street Journal recently reported that China's state-run China Aviation Industry Corporation may offer its AC-313 helicopter for use in the next Marine One fleet. The President of the United States of America should not be flying around in a helicopter that is made in China.

It was a $4 billion mistake to cancel the presidential helicopter program in the first place, but putting a state-run Chinese company in the running for the new project would be a slap in the face to American workers, and it would harm this industrial operation here in the United States, which we know is very much in need of the kind of attention that we need to give to it and the kind of energy that needs to be generated including a lot of jobs.

If the Chinese actually won the contract, our most sensitive national security information, the technology and systems we use to transport our president, could be put directly into the hands of a foreign power. I cannot imagine a worse mistake. I've urged Secretary Gates to consider these implications, and I hope that upon looking into the matter, that he will make the right decision.

So, brief conclusion. I thank the Commission for its dedication to the study of our relationships with China. For more than a decade, the Congress has benefited from your work, not just the Congress has benefited from your work, but as a result of the Congress' benefiting from your work, the nation has benefited from your work, and we are all deeply, deeply appreciative of the things that you have done.

So it continues. It continues, and the work that you do continues to be critically important, and for all of those reasons, I very much, very deeply appreciate the opportunity that you have given me to be here with you this morning and to say a few things about the kind of circumstances that I know you are dealing with effectively, and how all of us need to deal with effectively, in order to strengthen the economic circumstances of our country as well as aspects of the security operations of this country, which are absolutely essential for our future.

So, again, my deep gratitude to you. I deeply appreciate the opportunity to be here.

VICE CHAIRMAN SLANE: Thank you, Congressman, for your very helpful remarks, and we really appreciate your time. Thank you, sir.

MR. HINCHEY: Thank you. Thank you very much.

PANEL II – (continuation)

HEARING CO-CHAIR WESSEL: Dr. Naughton, if you had any thoughts on the questions I had asked earlier.

DR. NAUGHTON: A couple quick thoughts. Again, I agree with Derek Scissors, that the main problem here, most of these large state firms are not big exporters so they're not direct challenges on the export side.

They're a big problem in terms of restricting our exports, not just because of the regulatory barriers, but also because they then turn around and generate very high profits because they operate in protected markets, and they can use these--they actually don't need that much subsidy because they are pretty high-margin businesses themselves.

So it's ironic that China today after going into the World Trade Organization experiences remarkable economic boom showing, you would think, beyond a shadow of a doubt that it's in their interests to continue liberalizing and opening up, and yet their response to that seems to have been to try and extract additional benefits from crafting clever regulatory barriers that give them additional benefits.

So I think, like Derek, I think it won't work. But still we have to respond, and I think we're especially challenged to respond to these large state-owned enterprises as they start to expand overseas.

Now, so far, almost all of that has been energy related, and in a way energy is special. We see lots of state-owned companies operating in energy markets around the world, and it looks like it's something we just have to learn to live with. But as this expands beyond energy into other sectors, I think we need, we need a more explicit and careful policy about what we do and don't permit for state-owned firms in the United States.

I think we need a policy with greater reciprocity between the two countries and maybe a Bilateral Investment Treaty might be attainable as a way to establish some better set of ground rules that are consistent with further liberalization, which is certainly in our interests, but certainly that would be very, very challenging.

I just wanted to make one last quick point. Of course, our objective here is to focus on the state-owned sector. But I do want to say that we also have problems with the private sector in China. The Chinese government is capable of very sophisticated differentiation in terms of when they want to allow and support the private sector, including in lots of high technology start-up sectors, where in many cases, it's private firms that get generous subsidies from the Chinese government and are tough competitors.

So in some ways, that is a good thing about China, that it continues to experience a robust growth of the private sector, but for us in terms of crafting policies, it creates a whole additional set of challenges that we need to respond to.

HEARING CO-CHAIR WESSEL: Thank you.

I hope we have another round of questions. There are many follow-ups that flow from that, but I will cede my time.

VICE CHAIRMAN SLANE: Commissioner Shea.

COMMISSIONER SHEA: Yes, thank you, both, for being here.

I want to continue along this line of questioning. I agree with both of what you're saying, that it would appear that there's immense inefficiency, immense misallocation of resources in China. If you read the book called Red Capitalism, which recently came out, and it goes into the self-dealing between the state-owned banks and the state-owned corporate enterprises, —the Chinese economy looks like a house of cards that may eventually collapse.

But there are others who say it's such a huge country, China is such a huge country, there is such upside, there is such productivity enhancement that can be extracted, that the collapse is not going to come any time soon, that it can bear these inefficiencies.

I was wondering if you could explore that a little more? You touched upon it, and I would encourage, Derek, Heritage, it's one thing to say the Chinese economy is going to collapse, it's inefficient, there's misallocation of resources, not to worry, but that's 20 years down the road or 15 years down the road. It's having an impact today in the United States.

I know you came up with a very brief policy response, and I'd like you to describe that in greater detail, but I think it's important for Heritage and others to come up with appropriate policy responses that can be pursued today before the inefficiencies really begin to put a drag on the Chinese economy.

So I would like to throw that comment out to you, and if both of you would respond to it.

DR. SCISSORS: I guess I'll start. That's a fair statement. I actually think the stagnation rather than collapse, and I think it's sooner than 20 years.

Responding to the first part of your claim, there is a lot of upside potential in China, but they're moving away from that. They tapped it, and they tapped it for a good 20, 25 years of reform, and then they moved away. And it doesn't matter how much potential you have, we have an incredible amount of untapped potential in this country, you adopt the wrong policies, you don't tap it, and it's just still sitting out there and nothing happens.

So I'm pretty bearish on the current direction of the Chinese economy. They can change. They've changed before.

With regard to policy responses, part of this is how bad you see the problem. The Congressman just here was citing American jobs lost to the trade deficit. I just completely reject the link between if you run a trade deficit, you automatically lose jobs. It's just false.

Now, you can run, you can lose jobs in a trade deficit. You can actually lose jobs in a trade surplus. It depends on what industries you're talking about.

So, what I would say about our current economic problems is that they're self-inflicted, and the best way to deal with China is to fix our own problems. Why? We are much richer than them. We have much more productive workers, on the order of ten times more productive, than they do, and we have a much better set of physical resources to deal with, more water, more arable land, less pollution, more coal, more natural gas, all of it.

We have all the cards in this battle, and when you hold the better hand, you don't worry about the other side so much. So my first response on the policy side is we hold the advantage; let's use it properly.

My second is we need to focus, and that's why I made those a little bit catty remarks about the currency. To me, even if someone were to say, look, currency is the number one problem, that's where all our energy is going to go to, I might say okay, I completely disagree with that. But when I talk to my friends at Treasury, and they're going to the S&ED, they have eight things they want to do. No. Not going to work. That's just a recipe for a talk shop. You got to figure out what is the priority of the United States.

Is the priority of the United States reducing regulatory protection for state-owned enterprises? Is it opening China's capital account? Is it breaking the peg? Whatever it is, we have to focus.

So, one of the things that happens when you obsess over China instead of dealing with your own problems is you see 20 different things you want the Chinese to do, and that's probably fair, there are 20 different things we want them to do. We're not going to get them to do 20 things.

Two maybe. So part, I would say working on regulatory protection of state-owned enterprises. There are other answers that would be good answers, but I'd say U.S. policy has to focus with regard to China, and we have to remember we have the advantages. Let's fix our own house first.

COMMISSIONER SHEA: Thank you.

Dr. Naughton.

DR. NAUGHTON: In trying to puzzle out the great mystery of the Chinese economy because it's so complicated and has so many positive and so many negatives, and I think a lot of it is there are long time lags. And they've made a lot of extremely astute investments over the last 20 years.

HEARING CO-CHAIR WESSEL: Push your microphone.

DR. NAUGHTON: Sorry. They've made many very astute investments over the last 20 years that contribute to productivity growth with long lags of five and ten years. So they're still reaping the benefits of policy choices made in the '90s and the early 2000s.

I agree with Derek, in the future, they'll be paying the costs of foolish policy choices that are being made now, but that's not going to happen for awhile. I think for the next couple of years, the Chinese economy is going to continue to do relatively well, and their big dilemmas are going to come when so many of these new technology projects reach a point where they have to say, all right, we're going to continue to support this or we're going to pull the plug on something that's been a disastrous waste of resources, and then we'll see how capable they are of learning, of continuing learning, because they've been very good at learning so far.

But you worry that they have lost that ability to learn for political reasons, not for intellectual reasons.

COMMISSIONER SHEA: Thank you.

If there is another round, I'd like a question, please.

HEARING CO-CHAIR WESSEL: Okay. Chairman Reinsch.

CHAIRMAN REINSCH: Thank you.

I've got three questions I want to try to squeeze in so short answers, please, Derek.

[Laughter.]

CHAIRMAN REINSCH: The first one is you've both done a good job of explaining why their SOE policy is bad for us in the short term, bad for them in the long term. Can you say a few words about whether or not it's bad for them in the short term?

DR. SCISSORS: Start right now.

CHAIRMAN REINSCH: Go ahead. One at a time.

DR. SCISSORS: It depends on your goal. If their goal is to prop up ten percent growth, then it's not because investment is doing that for the time being. So, there a bunch of countries around the world who are in love with high growth. China is definitely one of them.

If their goal is efficient use of resources, including environmental resources, then they're hurting themselves even in the short-term. Short answer.

CHAIRMAN REINSCH: Okay. Barry.

DR. NAUGHTON: And it hurts them politically I think that it prevents them from evolving towards a more flexible, diverse economy and a more open flexible society, as well. So I think it hurts them in the short run, too.

CHAIRMAN REINSCH: Okay. Good arguments. I'm trying to marshal arguments to use prospectively. I think they've locked themselves into high short-term growth, and it's very difficult for them to move off of it for a variety of reasons, including political, and that's why this is an attractive option even despite the many problems.

I had an interesting conversation yesterday with someone who said that people he'd been having conversations with who had been in China recently had noticed a new development, and I just wanted you to comment if either of you have observed this. Foreign companies that are doing business in China are now discovering that when they meet with Chinese government officials to discuss whatever it is that they need to discuss, often a representative of the relevant SOE is in the room sitting at the table with the Chinese government officials, essentially making the SOE an instrument of government policy.

Have you heard this story?

DR. SCISSORS: Yes, I definitely have. That's part of what I made my opening remarks about. This is a two-way relationship now, whereas, before it wasn't. Ten years ago, the central government told the SOEs what to do. I don't mean to exaggerate--but now the SOEs want a seat at the table when these kinds of policy decisions are made, and they're pushing back and having some influence over central government policy that just didn't occur before they became these huge monstrosities.

CHAIRMAN REINSCH: You describe this relationship as two-way in the sense that both sides are leaning on the other.

It sounds like you also think that the government is paying attention to what the SOEs are telling them. Yes?

DR. SCISSORS: Yes, absolutely. I mean you're seeing, the way one of my friends--there's a reform branch in the Chinese government centered on the People's Bank. The way one of my friends in the reform branch said it's now one against two. We used to argue with the central government. Now, we argue with the central government and some giant firm who says this is going to hurt us; don't do that.

CHAIRMAN REINSCH: And they're finding that the SOEs' approach, not unlike companies everywhere, I suspect, is to take care of themselves and not be very interested in macroeconomic consequences.

DR. SCISSORS: What's good for PetroChina is good for China.

[Laughter.]

CHAIRMAN REINSCH: Sound bite of the day.

Dr. Naughton, have you run into the same phenomenon?

DR. NAUGHTON: Yes, definitely. And just in terms of personalities, we all remember back in the 1990s, Zhu Rongji had this very healthy skepticism of big entrenched companies and a willingness to stir things up and unleash competitive forces, and that was extremely healthy, and there's nobody like that today.

And so under those circumstances, then politically-connected families now have their people in the big state-owned firms, and they've all learned how to work the system, and it's a very worrisome political outcome.

CHAIRMAN REINSCH: Thank you.

Okay. Derek, a final question primarily for you, but if Dr. Naughton wants to comment, that's fine. This is from left field, but I think may end up being relevant. Are you familiar with this, as yet unpublished, Council on Foreign Relations work by Michael Spence that looks at the U.S. economy in terms of tradable and non-tradable sectors, and concludes that the job creation is all in the non-tradable sector?

What do you think of it?

DR. SCISSORS: I've seen summaries of it. I have not seen the report so, you know, big qualifier. That doesn't surprise me. What you'll also see is that the increase in productivity in the tradable sector is a lot higher than the increase in productivity in the non-tradable sector.

So what you've just got there is we have a section of the U.S. economy that's exposed to competition and becomes really efficient. And a section of the U.S. economy that's less exposed to competition and, by the way, gets a lot more in the way of government support and creates jobs on that basis, but is inefficient and, that's a tradeoff. And there is no way--I'm going to keep my answer short--there is no way we are going to get the more productive worker/more worker dispute settled in this, but that's really what Spence is showing.

CHAIRMAN REINSCH: By that logic, that would not mean anything has changed. That would be historically true as well as recently true; wouldn't it?

DR. SCISSORS: It would be historically true. You might see some intensification over time as you would expect with globalization, and the fact that in the '60s, globalization was about the U.S. makes everything because no one else knew how to make it as well as we do. That's not true now so you're going to see historical trend, but perhaps an intensification of that trend.

CHAIRMAN REINSCH: Yes. Thank you.

HEARING CO-CHAIR WESSEL: Commissioner Mulloy is next, but just a quick comment because the author of the study you disagreed with on the implications of the trade deficit with regard to jobs will be appearing before us later day, and hopefully he'll be able to identify his conclusions.

Commissioner Mulloy.

COMMISSIONER MULLOY: Thank you, Mr. Chairman. Thank both of our witnesses for their testimony today.

Dr. Scissors, whenever I'm out speaking, I always talk about the testimony you gave us about how the Chinese prop up the dollar, and that they buy our Treasuries and you said if they weren't buying our Treasurys, or I think now our companies, they would have to build a very big mattress because they got to get those dollars off the market; right? That was terrific testimony.

In your testimony today, on page three, you say "SOEs as a matter of course also receive hefty power and other input subsidies not available to genuinely private firms," making the point that these SOEs get a lot of benefits and subsidies from the Chinese government.

And then Dr. Naughton, you concluded your testimony by saying these SOEs present a big challenge for the United States.

I remember reading in a study where Huawei, the EU looked at Huawei, and I think that they said Huawei was receiving all kinds of subsidies from the Chinese government.

I wanted to ask you both a quick question and then a further question. Is Huawei a state-owned enterprise, in your judgment, Dr. Scissors and then Dr. Naughton?

DR. SCISSORS: In my judgment, it's absolutely a state-owned enterprise. I am not concerned with the background of Huawei's executives. It won't change its nature when they leave. I think that's a mistake.

The reference I would make is as follows: telecom has to be absolutely dominated by the state. Huawei is China's largest telecom equipment provider; it's the second-largest telecom equipment provider in the world on some measures. If telecom has to be absolutely dominated by the state, Huawei is a state firm. The end.

COMMISSIONER MULLOY: Yes. Do you have anything, Dr. Naughton?

DR. NAUGHTON: I think that is correct in terms of the policy implications, that we should understand that Huawei will have a very close and special relation with the Chinese government. It is not juridically a state-owned firm. It is an employee-owned private corporation, but, I think we fall into, we create too many difficulties for ourselves if we expect to say that there's a very clear line in all cases. This is a special case where you have a non-state firm that for very special reasons acts like a state firm.

COMMISSIONER MULLOY: It seems that it gets a lot of subsidies from the Chinese government; would that be correct?

DR. NAUGHTON: Well, it has a $10 billion line of credit from the China Development Bank, which helps.

COMMISSIONER MULLOY: Okay. That helps, yes.

DR. NAUGHTON: Yes.

COMMISSIONER MULLOY: Now then let me ask you further, in our CFIUS process, we make a distinction between a purchase of an American company by another private company, and a purchase of an American company by a government-owned entity, requiring a more searching analysis in the second case.

Do you both agree that that's a good test to have?

DR. NAUGHTON: I think that is appropriate, yes.

COMMISSIONER MULLOY: Doctor?

DR. SCISSORS: Yes. I think it's very appropriate and thank you for letting me do a little bit of an advertisement. The Heritage China Investment Tracker, which Dan Rosen is going to offer a feeble imitation of later today--Dan's a friend of mine, but he's a "Johnny come lately," and we have to be serious--points out that half of China's investment volumes since 2005 is for centrally-controlled state entities, two in oil, as Professor Naughton has suggested, CIC, which is one of the sovereign wealth funds, and Chinalco, which is a metals company.

So, if you care about Chinese investment in the U.S., you have to distinguish between state-controlled firms and private entities. Otherwise you're missing the boat.

COMMISSIONER MULLOY: All right. I have a further question. I was looking at the Canadian test for reviewing purchases by foreign entities of Canadian companies, and our U.S. test is it goes through unless you find there's a national security problem. The Canadian test is they review it and see if it would be a net benefit to Canada, and they list a number of factors.

I see all that Chinese government-owned money out there, and I see they're going to buy a lot of things in this country. Do you feel maybe we ought to consider looking at the Canadian test as maybe a more appropriate way to review this foreign investment coming into the country, particularly from state-owned enterprises? Have you thought about that or would you think about it?

DR. SCISSORS: I've thought about it a lot. To me, Australia also has a different test than we do, and they receive the most Chinese investment even though their economy is much smaller than ours.

So changing the test is not a sign that you're rejecting Chinese investment. If it were, I don't propose that. I don't want to unconditionally reject Chinese investment. I think that's a terrible mistake.

There is some ways in which CFIUS is too narrow. Equipment supply. We have the big deal with ZTE trying to win a large equipment supply contract. CFIUS isn't technically supposed to cover that.

So I would like to change CFIUS. I would like to make it more specific, including on the national security side. I think net benefit--in changing the test, it's going to depend on what you mention, sort of how you spell it out. The more specific, the more transparent, the better. So I want a broader scope for CFIUS, but I want it to be transparent and detailed rather than-- and I'm not suggesting that you said this--but if we had something like "we'll approve all investments that are a net benefit to the United States," that's scope for all sorts of problems.

COMMISSIONER MULLOY: Yes.   Dr. Naughton, did you want to comment?

DR. NAUGHTON: No. I have nothing to add to that.

COMMISSIONER MULLOY: Thank you. Thank you very much, both of you.

HEARING CO-CHAIR WESSEL: Thank you.

Commissioner Cleveland.

COMMISSIONER CLEVELAND: Thank you both for appearing this morning.

Dr. Naughton, you said early in your testimony that the debates about democratization are really about state-owned enterprise power. Can you elaborate on that a bit?

DR. NAUGHTON: Sure. I wouldn't want to go so far as to say they're really about it, but that there is a substantial sense of discomfort in China with the concentration of power, with the entrenched interest groups that are entangled with some of these large state enterprises, and there I did a recent piece where I quoted of all things a paragraph from People's Daily saying, we've reached a point where entrenched interest groups in our economy absolutely need to be confronted in order to continue the process of reform.

Amazing; right? And there was a period in 2010 when Premier Wen Jiabao was talking a lot about reform, and basically the main response outside China was "what is he talking about"? Because if he was talking about democratization and human rights, it was occurring at a time when the government he's presiding over was moving in exactly the opposite direction.

But I think it does make some sense to interpret this as a desire to tackle some of the privileges of some of these entrenched state-owned enterprises. They're often referred to as monopoly enterprises. They're not strictly monopolies but sort of oligopoly enterprises with the very high incomes that some of the people there make. Having them deliver dividends to the government can be seen as part of that. It's not a very satisfactory policy, but I think that is part of what's going on in Chinese debates.

COMMISSIONER CLEVELAND: Dr. Scissors, do you have anything to add?

DR. SCISSORS: Professor Naughton knows more about this than I do, I think. I tend to stay away from the political side because I have too much on my plate on the econ side, as I think maybe we all feel.

It is true that the battle has been--lines have been kind of extended. There was the political battle line of reform and the economic battle line of reform and seems like there is some mixing of the two now, which is why National People's Congress Chairman Wu threw in that privatization comment. That was not a mistake or an accident.

He was saying all of you people who want democratization forget it, and by the way, in my target are all of you people who want privatization too.

COMMISSIONER CLEVELAND: Dr. Scissors, you keep talking about regulatory reform. How and where would we pursue that?

DR. SCISSORS: Well, the first thing to do is to ask the Chinese, and ask them with a stick behind it, which is what are you talking about? When you say the state must absolutely control, when you say the state must lead, when you say central SOEs must be heavyweights, I want to know what that means.

How much of your market is open to everybody other than state-owned enterprises? And we need a specific answer, and if we can't get a specific answer--economists, we're all nerds. I admit it. We love transparency. But you got to start with that. Right? Even if they start with 90 percent. Forget it, all of you are fighting over ten percent of our 1.3 billion person market. Good luck with that.

You start with 90 percent, you have a basis for negotiation. Until, and Professor Naughton has already said this, they refuse to publish the document, and I have an explanation for why. They don't want to be caught pinned down by this in our talks. The first thing we got to do, if you think this is a serious problem or, as I think it is, the biggest problem, is get them to tell us what they mean by the central role of the state specifically.

Then you can talk about it, and then you can decide the level you're willing to come down to, 70 percent of the market, 51 percent of telecom, 75 percent of oil, that's unacceptable.

Once we know what we're dealing with, then you can make much, much better informed U.S. policy. So that's where I'd start, and then, after that, it's kind of speculation because we don't know what the Chinese are, their policy is on state dominance.

COMMISSIONER CLEVELAND: And how would you suggest pursuing that? Would that be a Secretary of Treasury initiative? What are the means by which we would pursue that?

DR. SCISSORS: If I were in charge, that's all we would talk about at the S&ED and the JCCT until they answer it, and I would put a time limit on it, and I'd say, look, if you can't answer this question, we can't deal with you. And you're not an effective cooperative economic partner.

I don't mean to say this is going to solve all our problems.

COMMISSIONER CLEVELAND: Right.

DR. SCISSORS: This is going to open the door to a new set of problems.

COMMISSIONER CLEVELAND: Right.

DR. SCISSORS: But we have to have that door open, in my opinion, and so that should be the first goal, not the ultimate goal, certainly the first goal of U.S. economic negotiations with the Chinese, and if they won't cooperate, that's a sign that we cannot deal with this particular government.

COMMISSIONER CLEVELAND: Do you think that there would be consensus within the American business community to focus on exactly what percentage of the market we really are talking about?

DR. SCISSORS: No. The American business community has proven itself repeatedly to be quite short-sighted as when they discovered indigenous innovation six years after it had first been implemented.

[Laughter.]

DR. SCISSORS: So, no. They should consider this a high priority because it's basically a statement to all exporters and foreign- funded firms operating in China, this part of the market is reserved for--you can't have it. And we don't know what that part is.

So the dreams of 1.3 billion consumers, you're not going to get that. What are you going to get? But I don't think that's what they would consider. I think the business community, while I agree with some of their concerns, tends to be a little bit too short-sighted, and as I said, this is a first step in a process, and they're not that interested in the process sometime.

COMMISSIONER CLEVELAND: Can you anticipate some of their objections?

DR. SCISSORS: Yes, they want to do something else; right? Basically, that does not lead to an immediate gain for my company operating in China.

COMMISSIONER CLEVELAND: Okay. Thank you.

DR. NAUGHTON: Maybe if I could just add two sentences here, too. Most American companies in China were very happy for 25 years to leave as many things as possible unsaid because that was where companies were going into new areas, and making windfall profits, and it's a deeply ingrained habit, and it worked really well for a long, long time.

So I think if you just saw the recent Beijing AmCham report, it's quite striking because something like 30 percent or 40 percent say that the direction of policy in recent years has been bad for them, and something like 75, 85 percent say their profitability is up, and they intend to expand their business.

So we've got some really complex situations to deal with here.

COMMISSIONER CLEVELAND: Okay. Thank you.

VICE CHAIRMAN SLANE: Commissioner Wortzel.

COMMISSIONER WORTZEL: Welcome back, Barry. It's good to see you. Derek.

I want to thank both of you for your testimony, and I know the focus of this hearing is on the big nationally-owned SOEs.

I've got some questions about other government-owned companies. When you talk about the SOEs, you refer to the 130 or so SASAC-managed companies, but a larger number of government-owned enterprises are owned by municipalities and provinces. There are about 114,500 provincially and municipally-owned enterprises as opposed to 130 SOEs.

And you've described how the SOEs are increasingly independent political actors that can exert political influence. I wonder if you could characterize how the municipally and provincially- owned enterprises interact with provincial and Party organizations and governments?

Are they also able to act as interest groups in their respective geographic locations? For instance, we were in Taiyuan a couple years ago; Taiyuan Iron and Steel is not on Cheng Li's list of state-owned enterprises, provincially owned, as far as I know.

But the general manager from 2000 to 2008 is now the Party Secretary of Taiyuan City and an alternate member of the Communist Party Central Committee. So are there provincial champions also that get special status and help from lower level governments, and do they get the same sorts of subsidies, and I guess, most importantly, if that's the case, should these factors be a consideration when the administration or any administration begins to categorize China as a market or non-market economy?

DR. NAUGHTON: A great question with many, many dimensions. So just a first quick overview. That sector is certainly very important, but it has continued to shrink, you know, even in recent years, as state ownership is re-stressed, still that local sector has continued to shrink, and I think that's mainly because it's much more exposed to competition than these big guys that we've been talking about for most of this session.

So it's very hard for the local governments to protect them, and they can't really erect trade barriers. They can create some regulatory friction, but there are limits to what they can do. Plus, from their standpoint, they are deeply involved in the management of these enterprises, but they can be deeply involved in the management of the enterprises and have them be private enterprises, too.

And if your cousin runs it, that's actually more efficient and more beneficial for you in a lot of ways. So I think that's what has really happened to the local state sector. It's much less important and it's much-- it looks much more private, but it's still so entangled with local political power. So it can be in some ways even more treacherous if you're trying to do business there because there are no rules but less of a macro problem in the way that we've been talking about.

DR. SCISSORS: I agree with that part. I'm going to try to answer your questions. See if I miss one. There have long been provincial champions. Usually the provincial champions were aimed at other provinces. Well, we're making cars here; you ain't bringing your cars in here; forget it. And so this is a long-established pattern. It has been mostly, in history, a block on Chinese internal economic integration.

I would say two things. One, a change I want to bring to people's attention. I think that Taiyuan Steel has now been bought out by a national steel company, and that's the consolidation that's going on in a bunch of sectors where the sector's disorderly market competition is to be reduced, and the way it's to be reduced is that the centrally state-owned enterprises are to absorb a lot of these provincial firms and make them national.

So you have 117 centrally state-owned SOEs, but the number of their subsidiaries is expanding as they grab up a lot of provincial firms in certain sectors, steel being one, coal, autos, et cetera.

With regard to what you were saying about treating China as a market economy, China is not a market economy, and I wish it were, to be back on the right track when we have to give up that designation. I don't think this is, and sort of agreeing with Professor Naughton here, I don't think this is the main reason they're not a market economy.

I do think that there are issues at the local level with local SOEs and state capture, but if that were what we were judging on, China would actually do better than if we take a more macro view where they are even further away from being a market economy.

DR. NAUGHTON: Can I add one, two quick sentences there? So thinking of these steel mills, the outcome is that national firms don't really consolidate that much of that industry. The concentration of the industry continues to decline, but the dysfunctional policy prevents a really efficient large-scale private firm from emerging. So it's a bizarre policy setting.

VICE CHAIRMAN SLANE: Commissioner D'Amato.

COMMISSIONER D'AMATO: Thank you very much, Mr. Chairman, and I want to thank the witnesses for their testimony and also the dialogue. I think this has been a very important session.

I find it ironic, in a sense, looking at the first page of your testimony, Dr. Scissors, in the historical sketch, the ten years prior to our supporting the Chinese accession to the WTO and giving them PNTR saw an expansion of the private sector and a reduction of the state sector. As soon as they got it, were admitted, they started moving in the other direction, and that seems to be accelerating, which is ironic.

My question is not different from what my colleagues have been saying, but I think it's important for us, and certainly our role in advising the Congress, to be thinking creatively about policy responses. The situation is obviously fairly clear, as you've laid it out.

The question is what kind of policy responses can be suggested by this Commission to the Congress to start moving in the other direction?

I've heard changes in the mandate and details of the CFIUS legislation. I've heard something about a new Bilateral Investment Treaty of some kind and some way that we can affect the regulatory system.

So my question really isn't much different from what I've heard from my colleagues, and that is as the--how do we encourage by our policy responses a trend toward more market economy development in China and to the implication of globalization as we understood it underpinning our commitments in the WTO?

We'd like, I'd like to know more about what kind of policy responses we can recommend that would be effective in starting to move the Chinese in the direction that underpins the theory of globalization and market economies that drove us to support their PNTR and the WTO.

DR. SCISSORS: Tough question obviously, but the right one. I'm going to use Professor Naughton's reference to a BIT, and again he made this comment, we all agree, trying to negotiate a BIT has about 25 different pitfalls you can fall into, but let's use it as an example.

If we were to have BIT negotiations with a carrot and a stick, the carrot is, hey, we're going to change CFIUS. We need to make it more transparent. We're going to change it in a way that's going to promote Chinese investment in the U.S., but only, only if we see China going back to the market reform track that it was on, but in 2002, and is not on now.

We use the BIT as a tool with a carrot. We have a lot of things the Chinese want to invest in here. They don't want to sink their money into quarter-percent Treasury bonds. That's just all they can do because there aren't markets open enough for them.

So we have a big carrot. We need to also have a stick. We can't rush into a BIT agreement. You can't make it on the basis of short-term needs. You can't even identify market access because what we saw in the WTO, as you brought up, is we--the WTO was a commercial agreement, and what we got was a change in the Chinese government, and it just nullified a lot of our commercial concerns.

We wanted to have 51 percent control of telecom ventures, and we had a big argument with them, and then the Chinese don't agree to any telecom joint ventures because they don't believe in it. Sorry. We need something more fundamental in the BIT. We do need to offer them a carrot, and we have a carrot. We also have to have a stick, which is if you want better access to the American market, and all of our natural resources and sharing in our manufacturing to some extent, excluding technology, we need to see you back on the reform path.

And then the hard part is we need to see you back on the reform path that isn't dependence on Zhu Rongji or somebody like him being in charge. That is a more fundamental change that doesn't have to do with the personnel of the current or future Chinese governments.

DR. NAUGHTON: And under the current circumstances in China, the big interpretation of the U.S. financial crisis has been to discredit in China the idea that need to stay on track to build an open market system.

So I think our ability to convincingly preach to them has, unfortunately, and it's really unfortunate, temporarily disappeared. Hopefully, it will return as they realize some of the implications of some of their policies, but I think in the short run, a stronger emphasis on reciprocity. We will do this. You want to invest in this in our country, fine, only if you give us reciprocal rights, because I think that language we can still communicate using those terms.

COMMISSIONER D'AMATO: Yes. What I'm hearing from you is that we have, we have something attractive to the Chinese, and that is their ability to invest in this market, and we should hold that to some kind of quid pro quo or series of quid pro quos that move them in the direction that we all understood they were going to be moving in.

DR. NAUGHTON: Yes. With the hope that a more open system for both of us is in both our interests. Yes.

COMMISSIONER D'AMATO: Thank you very much.

VICE CHAIRMAN SLANE: Commissioner Blumenthal.

COMMISSIONER BLUMENTHAL: Thank you very much.

I notice references, particularly in Dr. Scissors' testimony, to a private sector in China, and I wonder if you could describe to me what the private sector in China is? Does it exist? Can you actually be a private entrepreneur or a private businessman and not have to, to be generous, have good relations with the Party in order to get land or to get investment--do you have rights and your own property? Is there any way to not deal with the state?

Of course, in every country, you have to deal with the state to some degree, but is it really what we would think of as a private sector given how much you've described--both of you have described--that the Party actually owns or gives access to?

So in terms of getting your financing, keeping your property, finding your market, all the kinds of things, getting your licenses, can you describe that a little bit? What is the Chinese private sector?

DR. SCISSORS: My answer to that is there's absolutely a Chinese private sector. It's not as big as a lot of people want to claim, and that gets back to my first comment about conflating private and non-state when part of non-state are firms that have heavy state involvement, and we've cited a couple of them here.

What I would say, a more forceful answer to your question is you need to distinguish between the behavior of the firm and the market it operates in.

There are a lot of Chinese firms that are operating for profit. They tend to be small. They're in certain areas. We've talked about the areas they're not in. Those are the areas the state has to dominate. They're absolutely private firms. They're operating in a distorted market. They're operating in a market where they are besieged at all time; their property rights may be in question. They buy land, and then it's just taken away. Their technology is stolen, and their competitors are subsidized heavily in various ways. So the market they're operating in is heavily distorted.

That doesn't mean that there's no possibility of a Chinese private firm, as I define it. There are certainly Chinese entrepreneurs who are trying to make money that look very similar to American entrepreneurs, and one of the reasons we know that is that in 2008, they started screaming bloody murder that they were getting driven out by stimulus, and they were.

So the answer to your question is kind of paradoxical, which is the way we know that there are really Chinese private firms is that they're under siege, when we see that.

COMMISSIONER BLUMENTHAL: This is a difficult question. Is there a way to be an honest Chinese entrepreneur in the sense that the access is so controlled? As you say, it's distorted, which is probably generous in a sense. The amount of corruption in the market and so forth is built into the system, as far as I understand, in terms of being given access to credit, in terms of property, in terms of the rapaciousness of the state in general.

Is there a way that entrepreneurs have found to do that without having to form let's call it very close relationships with Party officials?

DR. SCISSORS: Well, if you're a big successful Chinese entrepreneur, then you have a lot of pressure to join the Party and play the game. If you become too visible, there would start being media articles around you and so on, but most of the millions and millions of Chinese firms are small. They don't have the option of like joining with the state because the state doesn't care about them. It would actually like them to disappear to a large extent.

So, yes, I see your point that there are some what people would call private firms that are conjoined with the state in some way, and I might not even call them private firms.

They're mom and pop operations. They make clothes. They have inputs to other sorts of production. They're not corrupted. They're just under fire and trying to survive.

The paradox is economists--what economists would cite out there is they're the efficient ones. When you're in a tough situation, you have to be really efficient. When you get every advantage, you don't have to be really efficient. So there are very efficient private firms in China, as well as the compromised sort of private firms that you're referring to.

DR. NAUGHTON: I very much agree with that. I might even push it a little further. There's a big private sector in China. It's not under siege. I mean, yes, they get discriminated against for sure, but it's growing rapidly. People are more and more used to just saying yes, it's private. There are a lot of dumb statements about non-state things that aren't private, that's true, but actually I think we can resolve those data issues, and you get a substantial, healthy private sector.

What you don't get is large-scale private firms playing a really dynamic role and getting really big. And that's a problem.

COMMISSIONER BLUMENTHAL: Thank you.

VICE CHAIRMAN SLANE: Thank you very much for all of your time, and we would ask you if you would be kind enough to respond to a few written questions we may have just to clarify some issues and expand on them? And we really appreciate your time. Thank you, gentlemen.

    We'll stand adjourned for ten minutes.

    DR. NAUGHTON: Thank you.

    [Whereupon, a short recess was taken.]

PANEL III: U.S. INVESTMENTS IN CHINA

    HEARING CO-CHAIR WESSEL: We'll get started with our next panel, and thank you, gentlemen.

    We have three panelists. This is regarding U.S. investments in China. Dr. Moran is the Marcus Wallenberg Chair in International Business and Finance at the School of Foreign Service at Georgetown University, where he teaches and conducts research on international economics, business, foreign affairs and public policy.

    Dr. Moran is founder of the Landegger Program in International Business Diplomacy, and serves as Director in providing courses on international business-government relations and negotiation.

    His most recent books include: Harnessing Foreign Direct Investment for Development; Does Foreign Direct Investment Promote Development?; and Foreign Direct Investment, Globalization and Developing Countries.

    Dr. Robert Scott is Senior International Economist and Director of International Programs at EPI, the Economic Policy Institute. Before joining EPI in 1996, Dr. Scott was an assistant professor with the College of Business and Management of the University of Maryland at College Park.

    His areas of research include international economics and trade agreements and their impacts on working people in the U.S. and other countries; the economic impacts of foreign investment; and the macroeconomic effects of trade and capital flows.

    Previously, Dr. Scott has testified at the Commission's 2005 hearing on "U.S. Trade and Investment Impacts on Pacific Northwest Industries," and as I mentioned with regard to our last panel, he is the author of papers looking at the impact of U.S.-China trade on employment patterns in the United States.

    Dr. Fung is a Professor of Economics at the University of California, Santa Cruz, and a co-founder of the Santa Cruz Institute for International Economics.

    His research areas are in international trade and finance, trade policies and multinational corporations, the WTO and the economics of the Asia/Pacific.

    Dr. Fung was a Senior Economist at the White House Council of Economic Advisors in both the Bush I and Clinton administrations, served as a U.S. government delegate to the OECD, and was an advisor--and I assume that's a typo--because it says OEDC, and I assume, Dr. Fung, it's OECD. And was an advisor and academic collaborator at the United States International Trade Commission.

He is also a Senior Research Fellow at the Hong Kong Institute of Economics and Business Strategy and an Associate Director of the Hong Kong Center for Economic Research.

Dr. Fung has also testified before the Commission, in 2004, on China as an emerging regional and technology power.

And we will begin in the order of introduction. Dr. Moran.

STATEMENT OF DR. THEODORE H. MORAN
MARCUS WALLENBERG CHAIR IN INTERNATIONAL BUSINESS AND FINANCE, SCHOOL OF FOREIGN SERVICE, GEORGETOWN UNIVERSITY, WASHINGTON, DC

DR. MORAN: Thank you very much for inviting me here.

My area of investigation is to try and examine what's the relationship between foreign direct investment in manufacturing in China and the increase of indigenous technological and managerial capabilities among Chinese firms, both state-owned firms and private firms.

So I've been looking at the question to what extent might foreign investors from the United States but also Japan, Korea, Europe, et cetera, be helping to propel China to be a technological superpower?

In particular, and I put this in the title of my presentation, is there a "Faustian bargain" of trading technology for access? So that this is a tradeoff to allow American or other foreign manufacturers in but force them to increasingly share the technological capabilities?

I'll be brief, but I have some good news and some bad news. I'll start with the bad news. China has been remarkably successful in designing industrial policies, joint venture requirements, indigenous technology regimes, technology transfer pressures, this whole mess of pressures on foreign multinationals, to create and reinforce indigenous national champions in high- speed rail transport, information technology, auto assembly, clean energy, and the emerging civil aviation sector.

That's the bad news. This Commission has focused several reports highlighting this and we have to keep at it. You have to keep at it and keep examining that. That's a very worrisome trend. That's the bad news.

Now, the good news. The good news is, and this is the area of expertise that I have been looking at, is how relatively thin this layer of forced technology transfer is. Despite the huge foreign manufacturing FDI inflows, the impact in China has been largely confined to the plants owned and controlled by the foreign multinationals, and this is particularly striking as the technology becomes more sophisticated and the skilled labor intensity grows up.

So that what you find is Chinese export profile has been transformed.

We all know this, but at the high end, this is almost exclusively controlled by foreign multinationals. Let me give you some figures, but you can look at this in much more detail in my written presentation, so that you find in high performance electronics, between 89 and 99--that's almost 100--99 percent of the high tech's exports are by foreign multinationals.

If you look at the Advanced Technology Products list, which again has been a subject that you have rightly been concerned with over the years, you find that 96 percent of all high-technology exports are done by wholly-owned, not joint venture, wholly-owned foreign multinationals.

I emphasize wholly owned because of the bad news that I led off with: companies don't want to share their technology or have a Chinese partner, so you find that this sector is actually very self-enclosed.

What about horizontal spillovers, vertical spillovers, development of supply chains? Are foreign multinationals transforming the Chinese economy through their backward linkages in supply chains? And the surprising answer is not much.

If you look over the past 20 years, not just ten years but 20 years, you find that the amount of domestic content and the skill level of the domestic content that's done in China has not been growing and is very small, is smaller than what you find in other states in Southeast Asia. The Malaysians have been much more successful, and the Thais have been much more successful, and the Mexicans and the Brazilians have been much more successful in developing backward linkages.

This has really become, remained much more of a foreign high-tech enclave. Again, if you look at chemicals, if you look at electronics, if you look at computers, the more sophisticated it is, the more it's controlled by multinationals, and the domestic content and domestic value added is small, and what has propelled the increasing sophistication is the inputs, which are imports from the United States, Western Europe, Japan, or Korea or India, so that you find an increase in sophistication of the inputs, but you don't find increased sophistication of the value-added within China.

I'm summarizing, I mean I'm trying to maintain eye contact because this is kind of different from what you hear, but what I find is that China has remained a low-value added assembler of more sophisticated inputs imported from abroad. So primarily a workbench economy, not a new Japan, not even a new Korea.

So now, why is this? Well, why is this is what we heard this morning: it's because of the distortions and the terrible doing-business climate within China. So that getting access to capital is hard, having your own intellectual property rights enforced is hard, your own contracts is hard, so that you don't really have the kind of robust domestic setting that you have, as I say, even in Penang or even in Brazil.

So it's very hard to gain, for the private sector or even the state-owned sector to gain traction being high-performance suppliers to the foreign manufacturing base.

My last point, which is more good news, but again somewhat, well, I'll look you in the eye and then explain to you how I come to this conclusion. Where do the gains from foreign direct investment in China when the foreign investors are successful, where do they end up?

I think all of us, and I've read Dr. Scott's testimony, I think he's a particular expert, it's very hard to track down where the profits, where the retained earnings, where the earnings from China, end up, the hiding places within the multinational system that generates it.

But I have employed a different methodology. I say if the MNC headquarters use earnings from China, like earnings from elsewhere, to fortify their position in world markets, what kind of activities will they fortify? And here I remind the Commissioners that we talk about globalization, and we talked about how worldwide corporations we have now, but U.S. headquartered MNCs have 70 percent of their operations, make 89 percent of their purchases, spend 87 percent of their R&D dollars, and locate more than half of their workers in the United States in the home economy.

Not much different for Germany, not much different for Japan, not much different for the UK. I mean despite the rhetoric of globalization, there is still the biggest footprint of multinationals is in their home economy.

So my concluding remark is we don't know exactly where these gains from investment in China go, but we do know where the footprint is that they end up, and they reinforce R&D spending, procurement and employment in the home economy.

Thank you very much.

[The written statement follows:]

PREPARED STATEMENT OF DR. THEODORE H. MORAN
MARCUS WALLENBERG CHAIR IN INTERNATIONAL BUSINESS AND FINANCE,
SCHOOL OF FOREIGN SERVICE, GEORGETOWN UNIVERSITY, WASHINGTON, DC

Foreign Manufacturing Multinationals and the Transformation of the Chinese Economy: Faustian Bargain to Trade Technology for Access?

I. Summary

What is the relationship between foreign manufacturing MNCs and the expansion of indigenous technological and managerial technological capabilities among Chinese firms?[15] How are foreign manufacturing MNCs changing the skill-intensity of activities and the extent of value-added of operations within the domestic Chinese economy? To what extent, might foreign direct investment be helping propel China to become an export superpower, "displacing Japan as the predominant economic power in East Asia", as Ernest Preeg declares, making the country

---

[15]This Statement draws directly upon *Foreign Manufacturing Multinationals and the Transformation of the Chinese Economy: New Measurements, New Perspectives*. Washington, DC: Peterson Institute for International Economics, Working Paper, forthcoming 2011.

the "economic hegemon" in the region? [16] Are multinationals "trading technology for sales in China"?[17] China has been remarkably successful in designing industrial policies, joint venture requirements, and technology transfer pressures to use FDI to create indigenous national champions in a handful of prominent sectors: **high speed rail transport, information technology, auto assembly, and an emerging civil aviation sector**. Prominent North American, European, Japanese, and Korean manufacturing multinationals rightly fear that they may find themselves launching rivals to their own market position when they weigh access to the vast Chinese market against technology acquisition and management imitation on the part of Chinese partners and other indigenous competitors.

Bringing in new technology to gain access to the Chinese market – whether for domestic market penetration or as a base for exports – may therefore often appear to individual foreign multinationals as making a Faustian bargain with the devil. "China can strike deals," asserts Steven Pearlstein, "that may provide short-term profits to one company and its shareholders but in the long run undermine the competitiveness of the other country's economy." [18]

But what is striking in the aggregate data is *how relatively thin* the layer of horizontal and vertical spill-overs from foreign manufacturing multinationals to indigenous Chinese firms -- and consequent export externalities -- has proven to be.

Despite the large size of manufacturing FDI inflows, the impact of multinational corporate investment in China has been largely confined to building plants that incorporate capital, technology, and managerial expertise controlled by the foreigner. Within this foreign firm-dominated production array, moreover, FDI payments for Chinese materials and labor used in the operations of the foreign plants have increased as domestic value-added has increased, as Nicholas Lardy shows.[19] But Robert Koopman, Zhi Wang, and Shang-Jin Wei find that the expansion of domestic content (and, conversely, decline in the import content) is concentrated at the low-skill intensive sectors of processing trade exports.[20]   As the skill-intensity of exports increases, the percentage of the value of the final product that derives from imported components rises sharply.

From a novel comparative perspective, the share of domestic value-added in FDI operations in China in high skill-intensive sectors such as computers and telecommunications ranges from *less than one-half to slightly more than one-half* of what is found in other developing countries where comparable measurements can be made, such as Mexico. Econometric analysis and survey data show that neither horizontal spillovers from -- nor strong and vibrant vertical supplier relationships to -- the vast FDI presence in China have yet taken place in any dramatic way, and difficult and complicated reforms are likely to be required before they do. These reforms include improving the doing-business climate for private Chinese domestic firms, submitting state-owned enterprises to competitive market forces, upgrading worker skills, creating engineering and managerial talent, reforming financial institutions, and improving infrastructure.

Across the expanse of the Chinese domestic economy, the accumulated evidence simply does not show FDI to be a powerful source for indigenous-controlled industrial transformation. In the case of exports, the production of increasingly sophisticated goods destined for international markets from China has been remarkably well

---

[16] Ernest H. Preeg.2008. *India and China: An Advanced Technology Race and How the United States Should Respond*. Washington, DC: Manufacturers Alliance/MAPI. p. 141-143, 69-71.

[17] David Barboza, Christopher Drew, and Steve Lohr. 2011. "Trading Technology for Sales in China". *The New York Times*. January 18, p. B-1.

[18] Steven Pearlstein. 2011. "China is following the same old script – the one that gives it all the best lines." *The Washington Post*, p. A-11. January 19, 2011.

[19] Nicholas R. Lardy. 2002. *Integrating China into the Global Economy*. Washington, DC: The Brookings Institution. Table 2-2, p. 38, and footnote 43.

[20]Robert Koopman, Zhi Wang, Shang-Jin Wei. 2008. How Much of Chinese Exports is Really Made in China? Assessing Domestic Value-Added when Processing Trade is Pervasive. *Op. cit.*

constrained to and contained within the plants owned and controlled by foreign multinationals and their international suppliers. China has remained a low value-added assembler of more sophisticated inputs imported from abroad – a "workbench" economy largely bereft of the magnified benefits and externalities from FDI enjoyed by other developing countries.

II.   Manufacturing Multinationals and Technology Capture in Headline Industries

Recent controversy about policies clustered under the rubric of "indigenous innovation" is only the most recent manifestation of Beijing's determination to use the lure of participation in the rapidly growing Chinese market – whether as a base for domestic sales or as a site for exports – to pressure foreign manufacturing multinationals to transfer industry best practices to Chinese partners and other Chinese firms in certain target industries.
In *high speed railroad transport*, the State Council, Ministry of Railroads, and state-owned train builders (China North Car (CNR) and China South Car (CSR), have been particularly successful in combining access to the Chinese domestic market, favorable financing, and competition among foreign investors to induce transfer of technology and production processes to Chinese national champions. In 2004, the Ministry of Railroads solicited bids to produce train sets that could reach 200 km/h. Alstom of France, Bombardier Transportation's German subsidiary, Siemens of Germany, and a Japanese consortium led by Kawasaki submitted bids, with all except Siemens winning part of the contract. Alstom teamed up with CNR's Changchun Railways Vehicles, while the Kawasaki-led consortium joined with CSR's Sifang Locomotive & Rolling Stock. The following year, Siemens won a contract to supply technology and build trains with CNR's Tangshan Railway Vehicle Company. The same strategy was success in transferring technology and production experience for key components. CSR Zhuzhou Electric obtained traction motor know-how from Mitsubishi Electronic. Yongji Electric obtained traction motor know-how from Alstom and Siemens.

In less than four years of "digestion", CSR mastered and improved what it received from Kawasaki, finally cancelling its cooperation agreement. According to Zhang Chenghong, the president of CSR , CSR "made the bold move of forming a systemic development platform for high-speed locomotives and further upgrading its design and manufacturing technology. Later, we began to independently develop high-speed CRH trains with a maximum velocity of 300-350 kilometers per hour, which eventually rolled off the production line in December 2007."[21]

Siemens and Bombardier remained active in China by signing a "cooperation agreement on joint action plan for the independent innovation of high-speed trains in China" with the Chinese Ministry of Science and Chinese Ministry of Railway to develop and build a new generation of trains with a top operations speed approaching 400 km/h, which came into service in late 2010.

On the basis of expertise acquired from joint ventures with MNCs in the Chinese market, Chinese firms have gone multinational themselves, either alone or alongside their international partners. Acting on their own, Chinese train-makers and railroad construction companies have signed agreements to build high speed railroad systems in Turkey, Venezuela, and Argentina, while bidding on high speed rail projects in Russia, Brazil (Sao Paulo to Rio de Janeiro), and the United States (Los Angeles to San Francisco). Teaming up with multinational allies first met in the home market, China Railway Construction Corporation joined with Alstom of France to win Phase I of the Mecca to Medina high speed rail line, while CSR has partnered with Siemens to bid on Phase II.

In *aerospace,* China similarly uses access to the Chinese market plus an informal "offset" policy to gain access to aviation technology and production expertise. Early in 2005, for example, China approached Airbus seeking an Airbus final assembly line to be built in China, and later in the same year signed a purchase order to import 150 Airbus A320s, worth approximately $10 billion.[22] Eighteen months Airbus later set up a joint venture company to

---

[21] Chen Biao and Zhu Huijue. "Era of 'Created in China' – an interview with CSR President Zheng Changhong." China Pictorial online. May 10, 2010.
[22] *Report to Congress of the US-China Economic and Security Review Commission* 2010. Washington DC: US   Government Printing Office, p. 99.

assemble the A320 in Tianjin, and an Airbus spokesman acknowledged a quid pro quo.[23] In 2009, the Airbus affiliate delivered the first mid-sized commercial airliner fully made in China.

For Boeing – as for Airbus – China's offset negotiations appear to have pushed the output from made-in-China requirements into international markets. While it is difficult to verify exactly what is involved in offset agreements because they are private agreements between purchaser and supplier, Boeing's website affirms that "Boeing is please to have been invited to help Chinese companies develop skills, achieve certification, and join world aviation and supplier networks….China builds horizontal stabilizers, vertical fins, the aft tail section, doors, wing panels and other parts on the 737; 747 trailing edge wing ribs; and 747-8 ailerons, spoilers and inboard flaps. China also has an important role on the new 787 Dreamliner airplane, building the rudder, wing-to-body fairing panels, leading edge and panels for the vertical fin, and other composite parts." On its Web site, Airbus reports that over half of its fleet worldwide contains components produced by Chinese companies.

As in high speed rail transport, international component companies have competed fiercely to supply inputs to Commercial Aircraft Corporation of China's C919 project which is designed to carry up to 200 passengers and compete directly with Boeing 737s and Airbus 320s.[24] The roster of US suppliers to the C919 includes Rockwell Collins, Honeywell, Hamilton Sundstrand, Parker Aerospace, Eaton Corporation, Kidde Aerospace, and General Electric. GE's joint venture with Aviation Industry Corporation of China (AVIC) in Shanghai will focus on domestic production of the electronics for communication, navigation, cockpit displays, and controls that constitute the constitute the avionics avionics "brain" for the new 787 Dreamliner of Boeing. "Doing business in China," opine David Barboza, Christopher Drew and Steve Lohr, "often requires Western multinationals like GE to share technology and trade secrets that might eventually enable Chinese companies to beat them at their own game – by making the same products cheaper, if not better."[25]

"What's good for GE or Honeywell or Rockwell is," claims Steven Pearlstein, "in this case, almost certainly not good for America and American workers." [26]

If the use of industrial policy to force technology transfer from foreign firms to indigenous companies is straightforward in high speed rail and aerospace, the results were initially quite counterproductive in the *automotive sector*.[27] Under the label of market-for-technology, Chinese policies from the 1980s into the 1990s offered foreign investors access to a high protected Chinese market in return for partnering with indigenous firms and promising to meet high domestic content requirements. Fearful of losing control over their intellectual property – as when the Chinese partner in the Audi-First Automobile Works "expropriated" the production technology after Audi's license expired in 1997 – international companies hesitated to introduce their most advanced technology into Chinese JV plants, and employed assembly processes that lagged world standards by almost ten years. After accession to the WTO, steady (albeit sometimes grudging) liberalization of the domestic market and rapid growth in internal demand allowed the major international auto companies to achieve economies of scale, rationalize production, and reach out to indigenous suppliers who themselves are able to enjoy full economies of scale. Help from foreign automotive investors in meeting the more stringent quality, safety, and anti-pollution standards may allow for expanding export opportunities to Europe and North America.

III. Manufacturing FDI in China and the Increasing Sophistication of Chinese Exports: Behind the Headlines

---

[23] *Ibid.*, p. 100.

[24] David Barboza, Christopher Drew and Steve Lohr. 2011. "GE to Share Jet Technology With China in New Joint Venture". The New York Times. January 17.

[25] *Ibid*.

[26] Steven Pearlstein. 2011. "China is following the same old script – the one that gives it all the best lines." *The Washington Post*, p. A-11. January 19, 2011.

[27] Guoqiang Long. 2005. "China's Policies on FDI: Review and Evaluation". In Theodore *H.* Moran, Edward M. Graham, and Magnus Blomstrom, eds. *Does Foreign Direct Investment Promote Development*. Washington, DC: Peterson Institute for International Economics, 2005).

Turning from sectoral case studies to aggregate data, there is no other way to describe the impact of foreign manufacturing investment in China except as massive. In 2003 China overtook the United States as the largest destination for foreign investment in the world, and then settled into second place. FDI inflows reached $168 billion in 2008, declining slightly to $143 billion in 2009.[28]

Multinational corporations in manufacturing have been the force that has propelled China's exports from low skill-intensive to high skill-intensive products. In 1992, the low skill-intensive sectors in China accounted for 55 percent of China's exports.[29] By 2005 these same low skill-intensive sectors' share had fallen to 33 percent. The composition of exports had shifted from a predominance of agriculture, apparel, textiles, footwear, and toys into machinery and transport products. Here the strongest export growth has been machinery, and within this broad classification telecom equipment, electrical machinery, and office machines constitute the largest shares. These more sophisticated sectors are dominated by processing trade, an arrangement in which imports are allowed into the country duty free where they are assembled for export. Processing trade exports of machinery and electrical products grew from $9 billion in 1992 to $323 billion in 2006, from 22% to 63% of all exports. Processing trade, in turn, is dominated by foreign multinationals (called foreign-invested firms or FIES, including both joint venture and wholly-owned affiliates of foreign multinationals), especially for more sophisticated products. The build-up of the foreign presence has been nothing short of remarkable.[30] In 1992, foreign multinationals accounted for 5% of exports in ordinary trade and 45% of processing exports. By 2006, foreign multinationals account for 28% of ordinary exports, but 84 % of processing exports. So today foreign multinational occupy a predominant place in processing trade, while maintaining a substantial presence in ordinary trade, too.

The share of processing trade – and the foreign firm share of exports -- climbs rapidly as the skill-intensity of the products increases.[31] For wearing apparel, processing exports as a share of industry exports in 2002 was 45.1 percent, with foreign firms accounting for 39.2 percent of industry exports. For household electrical appliances, processing exports as a share of industry exports was 79.1 percent, with foreign firms accounting for 56.9 percent of industry exports. For electronic devices, processing exports as a share of industry exports was 89.7 percent, with foreign firms accounting for 87.5 percent of industry exports. For telecommunications equipment, processing exports as a share of industry exports was 91.2 percent, with foreign firms accounting for 88.4 percent of industry exports. For computers, processing exports as a share of industry exports was 99.1 percent, with foreign firms accounting for 99.4 percent of industry exports.

So foreign manufacturing multinationals have been responsible for changing the composition of China's exports, but it is almost exclusively the foreign firms who are producing the more sophisticated exports.

The importance of this observation comes into clearer focus when examining China's growing presence in export of what are classified as "Advanced Technology Products".

The headline industry cases examined in the previous section, combined with China's rapid growth in Advanced Technology Products (ATP) to developed countries – leading, for example, to a Chinese surplus in ATP goods in China-US bilateral trade -- leads to speculation that China might be "leapfrogging" ahead technologically.[32] But Who-Is-Us? that have been engaging in Advanced Technology Exports from China?

---

[28] UNCTAD. *World Investment Report 2010*. Annex Table 1.

[29] Mary Amiti and Caroline Freund. 2010. "What Accounts for the Rising Sophistication of Chinese Exports?" in Robert C. Feenstra and Shang-Jin Wei, eds., *China's Growing Role in World Trade*. Chicago: University of Chicago Press for the NBER.

[30] Robert C. Feenstra and Shang-Jin Wei. 2010. "Introduction" *Ibid*.

[31] Robert Koopman, Zhi Wang, Shang-Jin Wei. 2008. How Much of Chinese Exports is Really Made in China? Assessing Domestic Value-Added when Processing Trade is Pervasive. NBER Working Paper 14109.

[32] Michael Ferrantino, Robert Koopman, Zhi Wang, Falan Yiung, Ling Chen, Fengjie Que, Haifend Wang. 2010. "Classification and Statistical Reconciliation of Trade in Advanced Technology Products: The Case of China and the United States" Joint Working Paper on US-China Trade in Advanced Technology Products. US International Trade Commission.

Foreign manufacturing investors have been responsible for more than 92 percent of all Chinese ATP exports since 1996, and 96 percent since 2002. And within this 96 percent foreign investor-dominated channel, there has been a shift to wholly-owned MNC exporters from joint venture companies. State-owned Chinese enterprises have an ATP trade deficit with the US, while private Chinese firms and collective enterprises contribute very little to ATP trade. And What-Is-Us? when the composition of Chinese Advanced Technology Exports and Imports comes under scrutiny?

The data show that there is a sizable technological gap between Chinese ATP imports and Chinese ATP exports. Chinese ATP imports from the United States consist of large-scale, sophisticated, high-valued equipment and devices, whereas ATP exports to the United States are small-scale products or components in the low-end of the ATP value-added chain.[33] Some 40 percent of the unit value ratios between US-exported ATP products and China-exported ATP products falls between 1 and 10 times greater for the US ATP exports to China, one-third falls between 10 and 100 times greater for the US ATP exports to China, and more than 13 percent are at least 100 times greater for the US ATP exports to China. In some categories, China simultaneously imports and exports the same product – for example, microscopes – but the types imported from the US cost ten to twenty times more than the types exported to the US, suggesting a sizable difference in features and capabilities.

I.   **Domestic Content and Value-Added in China on the Part of Foreign Multinational Exporters: A Comparative Perspective**

In processing trade where foreign investors are heavily represented, Nicholas Lardy shows that the import content of processing trade exports has steadily declined, overall, meaning that the domestic content and value-added in China have been on the rise.[34] In the first half of the 1990s the import content of processing trade exports was approximately 80 percent (domestic content 20 percent); by the late 1990s, it was around 65 percent (domestic content 35 percent). By 2007, the import content of processing trade exports was 60 percent, with domestic content 40 percent.

But Robert Koopman, Zhi Wang, and Shang-Jin Wei find that the decline in the import content is concentrated at the low-skill intensive sectors of processing trade exports.[35] As the skill-intensity of exports increases, the percentage of the value of the final product that derives from imported components rises sharply. For wearing apparel, the percentage of the value of the final product that derives from imported components is 62.4 percent. For household electrical appliances, the percentage of the value of the final product that derives from imported components is 76.3 percent. For electronic devices, the percentage of the value of the final product that derives from imported components is 85.2 percent. For telecommunications equipment, the percentage of the value of the final product that derives from imported components is 91.6 percent. For computers, the percentage of the value of the final product that derives from imported components is 96.1 percent.

Greg Linden, Kenneth L, Kraemer, and Jason Dedrick provide a fascinating look at who captures value in advanced electronics products exported from China, and where those who capture value are located.[36] Value-capture means the margin for the firm after paying for inputs and labor. Their target is Apple's iPod assembled in China with a retail price of $299 in 2005. In their estimation by far the most costly input in the iPod is the 30GB hard drive from Toshiba, which costs $73 or more than 50% of the total input cost, with a margin for Toshiba of about $20, which they assign to Japan. The second-most valuable input is the display, with a factory price of $20, plus

---

[33] *Ibid.*

[34] Nicholas R. Lardy. 2002. *Integrating China into the Global Economy*. Washington, DC: The Brookings Institution. Table 2-2, p. 38, and footnote 43.

[35] Robert Koopman, Zhi Wang, Shang-Jin Wei. 2008. How Much of Chinese Exports is Really Made in China? Assessing Domestic Value-Added when Processing Trade is Pervasive. *Op. cit.*

[36] Greg Linden, Kenneth L, Kraemer, Jason Dedrick. 2007. "Who Captures Value in a Global Innovation System? The case of Apple's iPod" Working paper. Personal Computing Industry Center, University of California, Irvine, June.

margin of $6 for Toshiba-Matsushita, which they again assign to Japan. Next are two microchips from US companies, Broadcom and PortalPlayer, leading to $7 in margin assigned to the US. The SDRAM Memory comes from Samsung, with $0.67 assigned to Korea. There are more than 400 additional inputs, with values from $4 to fractions of a penny. Apple's gross profit meanwhile is $80, or $155 if distributed through Apple's own retail outlet. The margins for the companies involved in the creation of the iPod (above costs of materials and labor) total $190: $163 accrue to the US, $26 to Japan, $1 to Korea, if the iPod is sold in the US. Some portion of $75 allocated to retail and distribution would go to other players if the iPod were sold outside the US.

Linden, Kraemer, and Dedrick conclude that "the value added to the product through assembly in China is probably a few dollars at most" (the popularly accepted figure is $4). They argue that while Apple's margins are high within the electronics sector, the "geography" of value-capture for the iPod is fairly representative for the industry.[37] Robert Koopman, Shi Wang, and Shang-Jin Wei support this contention with their finding that Japan, the United States, and Europe (EU15) are the main sources of foreign content for computers and electronics in China, accounting for about 60% of imported components.[38]

In 2010, Yuqing Xing and Neal Detert undertook a similar calculation of the value-capture in China in assembly of Apple's iPhone.[39] They find that the value-added in China in 2009 for the iPhone was $6.50 per unit, which was 3.6 percent of the total shipping price of the phone.

At the end of the day, China's high tech export explosion represents multinational corporations bringing high skill-content high value-added inputs into China, assembling them into final products (or semi-assembled intermediates), and exporting them to world markets.[40]

Other comparative analytics substantiate the modest outcome China has achieved in using foreign multinationals to upgrade the indigenous industrial base. From a comparative perspective, the share of domestic value-added in FDI operations in China in high skill-intensive sectors such as computers and telecommunications, for example, ranges from *less than one-half to slightly more than one-half* of what is found in other developing countries where comparable measurements can be made, such as Mexico.

This comparative evidence comes from Justino de la Cruz, Robert B. Koopman, Zhi Wang, and Shang-Jin Wei who are able to compare the outcome of manufacturing FDI in China rigorously to other developing countries where there are similar processing-trade regimes.[41] The most accurate comparison can be made with Mexico where the maquiladora and PITEX (Program of Temporary Imports to Produce Export Goods) structures resemble China's processing-trade system.

In low-skill intensive industries – such as apparel – the FDI-dominated processing industries show a relatively large share of domestic value added in both countries: a 35.4% share for Mexico, a 37.6% share for China.

In the middle-skill intensive automotive sector, the FDI-dominated processing industries show what De La Cruz,

---

[37] *Ibid.*, p. 10

[38] Robert Koopman, Shi Wang, and Shang-Jin Wei . 2009. "A World Factory in Global Production Chains. Estimating Imported Value-Added in Chinese Exports", UK: Center for Economic Policy Research, Discussion Paper 7430, September.

[39] Yuquing Xing and Neal Detert. 2010. "How the iPhone Widens the United States Trade Deficit with the People's Republic of China" Tokyo, Japan: Asian Development Bank Institute. ADBI Working Paper Series, No. 257. December.

[40] Lee Branstetter and Fritz Foley note that US MNCs export very little of what they produce in China back to the US. Stephen Yeaple amends this to point out that US MNC exports to other countries in the region, perhaps for integration into final products elsewhere, is growing rapidly. Lee Branstetter and C. Fritz Foley. 2010. "Facts and Fallacies about US FDI in China (with Apologies to Rob Feenstra)". Stephen Yeaple. "Comment" in Robert C. Feenstra and Shang-Jin Wei, eds., *China's Growing Role in World Trade.* Chicago: University of Chicago Press for the NBER.

[41] Robert Koopman, Zhi Wang, Shang-Jin Wei. 2008. How Much of Chinese Exports is Really Made in China? Assessing Domestic Value-Added when Processing Trade is Pervasive. NBER Working Paper 14109. Table 5. Justino de la Cruz, Robert B. Koopman, Zhi Wang, and Shang-Jin Wei. 2010. "Estimating Foreign Value-Added in Mexico's Manufacturing Exports". Working paper. Tables 7and 8. Justino de la Cruz, Robert B. Koopman, Zhi Wang, and Shang-Jin Wei.2009. "Domestic and Foreign Value-added in Mexico's Manufacturing Exports, power points, May 9.

Koopman, Wang, and Wei characterize as "medium" domestic value added in both countries: a 35.2% share in motor vehicles and 23.9% share in auto parts for Mexico, a 33.8% share in motor vehicles and a 28.7% share in auto parts for China – although Mexico scores a much higher 43.8% domestic value added share in "other transportation equipment" (for which there is no comparable category in the authors' data for China). For China, Nicholas Lardy notes that for some vehicle lines the domestic content has been climbing over time: the popular Santana, produced by a joint venture between Volkswagen and Shanghai Automotive, was launched in 1985 with a domestic content of 2 percent but recorded domestic content well over 90 percent by the late 1990s.[42] Other large volume production vehicles, such as the Buicks produced by GM and Shanghai Automotive, followed a similar track.

For high skill-intensive sectors, such as computers and telecommunications equipment, both countries have a much lower share of domestic value added in the FDI-dominated processing sectors. But, as noted above, Mexico's small domestic value added share (8.5% share in computers, 14.9% share in telecommunications) is nonetheless almost twice as large to well more than twice as large as the shares for these industries in China (3.4% share in computers, 8.4% share in telecommunications).

Turning from measurement of domestic content within foreign-owned factories to measurement of impact from FDI on surrounding firms within China, econometric assessments of horizontal and vertical spillovers from multinational investors to indigenous Chinese firms (private or state-owned) appear to be relatively weak in comparison to other countries in Asia, as do export externalities. The reasons include lower pay at Chinese companies and brain-drain from them to foreign MNCs, gaps in technology and quality-control standards, adaptability limitations, and intercultural communication problems.

Bruce Blonigan and Alyson Ma investigate the extent to which Chinese domestic firms are "keeping up" or even "catching up" with foreign exporters.[43] They do not try to measure spillovers directly. Instead, they compare the volume, composition, and quality of exports of the two groups. They find that the general pattern over the time period, 1997-2005, runs exactly counter to what one would expect if Chinese firms were catching up – foreign firm's share of exports by product category and foreign unit values relative to Chinese unit values are increasing over time, not decreasing. *Chinese exporters are not even "keeping up" let alone "catching up" with foreign multinational investors in China.*

To deepen the impact of foreign investment on the indigenous economic base in China – expanding the linkages from international investors and deriving more spillovers from their presence – will require improving the doing-business climate for private Chinese domestic firms, submitting state-owned enterprises to competitive market forces, upgrading worker skills, creating engineering and managerial talent, reforming financial institutions, and improving infrastructure. Many of these reforms are underway, to a greater or lesser extent. So positive contributions from foreign manufacturing multinationals to the indigenous Chinese economy -- beyond the 13-14 million workers directly employed in foreign MNC plants -- are likely to increase over time. Thus far, however, the aggregate data simply do not show FDI to be a powerful source for indigenous-controlled industrial transformation in China.[44]

Where do the gains from FDI in China end up?

[42] Personal communication, November, 2010.

[43] Bruce A. Blonigen and Alyson C. Ma. 2010. "Please Pass the Catch-Up: The Relative Performance of Chinese and Foreign Firms in Chinese Exports" in Robert C. Feenstra and Shang-Jin Wei, eds., *China's Growing Role in World Trade*. Chicago: University of Chicago Press for the NBER.

[44] Lee Branstetter and Fritz Foley note that US MNCs actually do relatively little R&D in China (three tenths of one percent of their worldwide R&D and less than 13 percent of their R&D performed in the Asia-Pacific region), and most of R&D activity in China appears to consist of customizing innovations discovered elsewhere for the Chinese market. Lee Branstetter and C. Fritz Foley. 2010. "Facts and Fallacies about US FDI in China (with Apologies to Rob Feenstra)" in Robert C. Feenstra and Shang-Jin Wei, eds., *China's Growing Role in World Trade, op. cit.*

In their dissection of the "value-capture flows" for Apple's iPod -- that demonstrates no more than $4 of the final sales price of $299 (2005) remains in China -- Greg Linden, Kenneth L. Kraemer, and Jason Dedrick suggest that the value-added attributed to the parent company that contributes a component or performs an integrative function to a product in China flows directly back to MNC headquarters. This is almost surely too simplistic -- especially for US MNCs -- given the American territorial tax system with the foreign tax credit and deferral that encourage US MNCs to use transfer pricing to keep accumulations of earnings offshore.

Rather than try to track down capital flows and hiding places within integrated MNC networks, the more sensible approach is to ask a slightly different kind of question: *if MNC headquarters use earnings from China, like earnings from elsewhere, to fortify their corporate position in world markets, what kinds of activities will those earnings help maintain or expand, and where will they be located?*

In coming to an answer for this question, it is striking to note -- even in today's globalized world – how remarkably home-based MNCs from developed countries have remained.

For the United States the most recent data show that US-headquartered MNCs have 70 percent of their operations, make 89 percent of their purchases, spend 87 percent of their R&D dollars, and locate more than half of their workforce within the US economy This predominant focus on the home economy has persisted over time, and changes only very, very slowly at the margin.

The home-market-centered orientation for MNCs across the developed world is not dissimilar.

Thus, while manufacturing MNCs may build plants in China -- or shift production to Vietnam, outsource to Mexico, take a chance in Costa Rica or the Czech Republic, develop a new application in Israel -- the largest impact from deployment of worldwide earnings is to bolster their operations in their home markets.

STATEMENT OF DR. ROBERT E. SCOTT, SENIOR INTERNATIONAL ECONOMIST AND, DIRECTOR OF INTERNATIONAL PROGRAMS, EPI, WASHINGTON, D.C.

DR. SCOTT: Thank you, Commissioner Wessel, Vice Chair Slane, other members of the Commission, for the chance to testify here today.

As you have heard, I have estimated that growing trade deficits have cost the U.S. 2.4 million jobs between 2001 and 2008. I'll be happy to defend that number later.

More than two-thirds of the jobs we've lost have been in the manufacturing sector, and, in my view, growing trade deficits with China represent the greatest threat to the future health of U.S. manufacturing.

FDI has played a key role in the growth of China's manufacturing sector. China is the largest recipient of FDI of all developing countries. It's the third-largest recipient of FDI in the world in the last three decades, trailing only the U.S. and UK.

Foreign invested enterprises, according to China's own statistics, are responsible for 55 percent of China's exports and 68 percent of its trade surplus.

While FDI slowed in China in 2009, it recovered strongly in 2010. It's up by 35 percent. I want to emphasize just four main conclusions and focus primarily here on policy responses that we might develop. I have a lot of analysis in the testimony we can talk about later as well.

While U.S. MNCs are responsible for a small share of FDI in China, FDI from the U.S. and other developed countries in the OECD has played a disproportionately large role in the rapid growth of GDP in productivity and exports in China.

In addition, data suggests that investment from U.S. MNCs could be as much or more than 16 percent of all FDI in China. As we have heard this morning, China has used a number of activist policies to attract and retain FDI and to maximize the benefits they receive from these.

The most important was the devaluation of the RMB by 57 percent between July of '86 and January of '94. The RMB was fixed at that level until July 2005.

And the best estimates is that the RMB is still 25 to 40 percent undervalued, which makes China, of course, an increasingly attractive place to export goods, and it makes exports from China super competitive both in United States and in other world markets. It's also a barrier to U.S. exports to China.

China has also provided tax holidays, incentives and Special Economic Zones, and billions of dollars in illegal subsidies to core industries and sectors, such as steel, glass, paper, and of course now the new green technology industries we've heard about.

Taken as a whole, China's FDI promotion regime has provided massive subsidies to these enterprises, which has encouraged firms to outsource production from the U.S. and other developed countries to China and has severely suppressed U.S. exports to China and the world.

My fourth point is that the U.S. should adopt new policies to level the playing field between the U.S. and China. Our emphasis should be on defending and recovering production in the United States and to maximize production and employment here.

These policies should benefit the United States Support for headquarters of multinationals should be at most a secondary concern, and I differ with Professor Moran on the benefits of those multinationals. I would point out that both U.S. and foreign multinationals have large and growing trade deficits with the United States, which does displace employment here.

In terms of policy responses, I'll note that our fair trade laws have become decreasingly useful, in part because of the growth of outsourcing and foreign direct investment abroad. It's just, it's very, very difficult to find domestic firms willing and able to file antidumping and countervailing duty cases in the U.S. The best illustration of that is the collapse in the number of law firms who pursue these cases.

The trade bar has been decimated in the last ten years because of the decline in the number of these cases. Someone needs to fill that gap because clearly China is still subsidizing and dumping products here in the United States.

So how should we respond? First, we need to take actions against China's currency manipulation, and here I would endorse the Fair Trade Act of 2011, which was also approved by the House in earlier version authored by Representatives Ryan and Murphy in the last Congress. The Ryan-Murphy bill was not, however, approved by the Senate in the last session of Congress.

I would suggest Congress reauthorize Super 301 which expired when we entered the WTO.

I think we should look at several alternatives for self-initiation of dumping and countervailing duty and other fair trade enforcement cases, including establishing an independent agency like the International Trade Commission that would investigate and could file such cases.

Congress could also consider chartering and funding an organization that recommended cases to Congress for action.

We've already heard about the recent rulings from the WTO regarding the treatment of China as a non-market economy and also the fact that, two things, in particular:

One, that this ruling determined that that state-owned enterprises were not necessarily public bodies, and so we couldn't just assume that they were delivering subsidies in countervailing duty cases.

And, of course, this case also ruled that we couldn't add countervailing duties and dumping duties together, and so that has been stricken from the options available to the U.S.

We need to amend U.S. trade law to find new ways to address these issues. I think also I believe at some point we're going to have to consider withdrawing from WTO dispute settlement processes. The deck seems to be increasingly stacked against the United States.

As Commissioner Wessel mentioned, the rules on China's treatment as a non-market economy expire in 2016. We need to address that issue. Clearly, China is a non-market economy, as we heard in the last session, and that needs to be addressed in some way. The WTO rules need to be revised to take that into account.

I have a number of recommendations regarding collection of additional data on the operations of multinationals and on the way in which they're financed. Those are all spelled out in my testimony and I would welcome questions on those later.

I would finally close with a plea for more funding for research on the operations of multinationals and on the impacts of international trade on the domestic economy. In this kind of research, data collection and improved access for researchers is key; better data will lead to better trade policy and trade enforcement, and that will improve the U.S. trade balance, which will generate jobs and tax revenues. So small investments in data collection can have big benefits for the country as a whole and can reduce both our trade and budget deficits as well.

Thank you.
[The written statement follows:]

PREPARED STATEMENT OF DR. ROBERT E. SCOTT, SENIOR INTERNATIONAL ECONOMIST AND, DIRECTOR OF INTERNATIONAL PROGRAMS, EPI, WASHINGTON, D.C.

Summary

Good morning Vice-Chair Slane, Commissioner Wessel and other members of the Commission and staff. Thank you for the opportunity to testify here today. Growing U.S. trade deficits with China cost the United States 2.4 million jobs between 2001 and 2008 alone (Scott 2010b). More than two-thirds of the jobs displaced were in the manufacturing sector, and growing trade deficits with China are the greatest threat to the future health of U.S. manufacturing.

Foreign Direct investment has played a key role in the growth of China's manufacturing sector. China is the largest recipient of FDI of all developing countries (Xing 2010), and is the third largest recipient of FDI over the past three decades, trailing only the United States and the United Kingdom (Table 2). Foreign Invested Enterprises (both joint ventures and wholly owned subsidiaries) were responsible for 55% of China's exports and 68% of its trade surplus in 2010, as reported by China.[45] While FDI in China slowed in 2009 as a consequence of the global recession, it recovered strongly in 2010, increasing $27.5 billion (35.2%). In my remarks today I will emphasize four main conclusions:

- While U.S.-based MNC's are responsible for a relatively small share of total FDI in China, FDI from the U.S. and other developed countries (in the OECD) has played a disproportionately large role in the rapid growth of China's GDP, productivity and exports. In addition, published academic research and data reviewed here suggests that MNCs from the United States may be under-reporting FDI in China. Under-reporting of FDI by U.S. MNEs should be addressed by officials and researchers from the U.S. Bureau of Economic Analysis (see specific policy recommendations, below).

- China has used a number of activist policies to attract and retain FDI, and to maximize exports and other benefits received from these facilities. First, the RMB (yuan) was devalued by 57.2% between July of 1986 and January of 1994, primarily in three distinct moves (Figure 2), and held at this level until July 2005. The best estimates are that the RMB is still 25% to 40% undervalued (Cline 2009 and 2010). China's currency manipulation is illegal under the GATT/WTO agreements and the IMF charter, as well as U.S. law (Scott and Bivens 2006). Currency manipulation dramatically lowers Chinese production costs and provides an effective subsidy to Chinese exports; it also acts as a barrier to imports from other countries. Second, China provided tax holidays and has offered FIEs preferential tax rates for corporate profits, and reduced value added tax rates.[46] China has also offered other incentives to MNEs that established subsidiaries and joint ventures in its "Special Economic Zones" (Xing 2010). Finally, China has provided tens of billions of dollars of illegal subsidies to firms in industries such as steel, glass, paper and new green technology industries.[47] Most of these incentives and subsidies are illegal under the terms of the WTO and U.S. fair trade laws.

---

[45] Ministry of Commerce, China (2011) and Invest in China (2011).

[46] Some or all of these tax preferences were phased out under the terms of a new Chinese Law in 2008 (Du, Harrison and Jefferson 2011). However, existing FIEs were allowed to retain some of the benefits offered prior to the passage of the new law. New tax rates for FIEs will be phased in until 2012, and firms granted tax holidays will continue to benefit until the expiration of those agreements.

[47] Haley (2008, 2009, 2010) and Scott (2010 and 2011).

- Taken as a whole, China's FDI promotion regime has provided massive, illegal subsidies to MNEs from the United States and other countries. These subsidies have encouraged firms to outsource production from the United States and other developed countries to China; they have contributed to the rapid growth of China's exports to the U.S. and the world; and they have severely suppressed U.S. exports to China, and to the world (China is now the most important competitor for U.S. exports on world markets).
- The United States can and should adopt new policies to level the playing field between the U.S. and China. Trade and manufacturing policies should be used to defend and recover production in the United States, and to maximize production and employment in U.S. manufacturing establishments. These policies should emphasize the benefits of U.S. production and employment. Support for the headquarters operations of domestic or foreign MNEs should be, at most, a secondary concern of domestic trade policies.

Enforcement of important U.S. fair trade laws, such as anti-dumping and countervailing duty (CVD) measures, requires a qualifying group representing domestic producers or workers that generate at least 25% of domestic volume of the like product to file a legal complaint. Litigation of these cases can cost millions of dollars, with uncertain outcomes—many such cases are rejected.[48] As U.S. industries have offshored production, and become increasingly dependent on low-cost foreign suppliers, their interest in filing fair trade complaints has declined. U.S. firms investing in China such as GM, Motorola, Johnson & Johnson, and the Blackstone Group, and large retailers such as Walmart, Target and CVS benefit directly or indirectly from China's currency manipulation and subsidies. These firms are more likely to threaten or otherwise discourage their suppliers from participating in fair-trade enforcement cases. Thus, fewer and fewer trade cases are being filed, simply because of the costs and difficulty of obtaining the support of a qualifying domestic injured party.

Specific policies that should be considered include:
- o Policies that threaten to impose strong sanctions on China for its illegal currency manipulation such as the Fair Trade Act of 2011, co-sponsored by Senators Brown and Snowe and Representatives Ryan and Murphy, and the much tougher Schumer-Graham currency reform measure adopted by the Senate in 2005.[49]
- o The Congress should re-authorize the Super 301 provisions in U.S. Trade Law, which required the USTR to initiate negotiations with priority countries to eliminate trade practices that impeded U.S. exports, including currency manipulation.[50]
- o The U.S. should establish an independent agency to pursue violations of U.S. unfair trade law, including illegal tax subsidies and other types of direct and indirect subsidies.[51]
- o Congress could consider chartering and funding an independent organization, like the Congressional Budget Office, that could investigate and file unfair trade complaints on behalf of Congress, or could refer complaints to committee for consideration of Congressional action.
- o Recently, a WTO appellate body ruled that the U.S. cannot simultaneously apply antidumping and CVDs to products imported from China under its non-market economy rules when imposition of such duties would amount to double-counting, that is, when the prohibited subsidy has

---

[48] The Congress and USTR can self-initiate some trade cases. However, this option is rarely used.

[49] The Ryan-Murphy bill which passed the House in 2010 would allow the Commerce Department to consider currency manipulation as a subsidy in CVD cases. This proposal would affect a small share of imports from China (at least initially). The Schumer-Graham 2005 amendment would have imposed a substantial (27.5%) across-the-board tariff on imports from China.

[50] The U.S. agreed to eliminate Super 301 investigations when the WTO was formed in 2004, under the Uruguay Round trade agreements.

[51] A direct subsidy could include, for example, below-market pricing for energy and raw materials. An indirect subsidy would be obtained by a firm in China that purchased subsidized materials, such as steel and glass made with subsidized energy and raw materials.

contributed to the below-market pricing that is the subject of the anti-dumping margin.[52] This ruling also sharply limited the definition of a "Public Body" (which can deliver subsidies), and rejected claims that State Owned Enterprises (SOEs) "exercised governmental functions on behalf of the Chinese Government." This ruling will sharply limit the ability of the United States to impose Countervailing Duties in cases involving Chinese subsidies. U.S. fair trade law may have to be amended to provide new legal and economic approaches to the assessment of countervailable subsidies that do not affect subject-import prices, and to address the role of SOEs. As an alternative the United States may wish to rethink its commitment to and participation in the WTO dispute settlement mechanism. The U.S. has lost several high-profile cases in recent years[53] and there is a growing perception that WTO appellate judges are choosing "to substitute their own views for the rules negotiated by the WTO parties" (Otteman 2011). The costs of participation in WTO dispute resolution may have begun to exceed its benefits and it may be time for the U.S. to withdraw from the dispute settlement process.

- Rules contained in the 2001 US-China WTO accession agreement regarding treatment of China as a non-market economy (NME) will expire at the end of 2016. These rules allowed U.S. petitioners in antidumping cases to treat China as a NME, which presumes that most prices are administered by the state. Comparable home prices for subject products are constructed based on prices in a third country. Rules governing application of the NME status will then revert to the WTO standard in 2016.[54] Domestic petitioners will be required to prove that "all domestic prices are fixed by the State." Otherwise, prices in China will be used as a basis for anti-dumping cases, which will favor producers in China (who benefit from many low, administered input prices). China is a mixed economy and manages many, but not all, domestic prices in most cases. The WTO NME rules are clearly defective in this case, and should be revised to allow treatment of China as a NME. If WTO members fail to approve these changes, this will provide another reason why the United States should consider withdrawing from the WTO dispute settlement process.

- U.S. manufacturing is falling farther and farther behind; China became the largest exporter in the world in 2009 (Figure 6)[55], and recently passed the United States to become the largest manufacturer in the world. One reason for this is that the United States lags far behind other countries in the use of industrial policies and other types of economic development initiatives, such as workforce development and training, publicly supported R&D, and also the use of preferential public procurement policies. China, in particular, is not a signatory to the WTO government procurement agreement. Other OECD countries who are signatories still manage to use government procurement to support domestic industrial development, for example through military offset programs (Herrnstadt 2010). The U.S. needs to develop a wide range of economic

---

[52] Full disclosure: I have appeared as a witness for domestic producers of steel pipe in a number of antidumping and CVD injury investigations before the U.S. International Trade Commission over the past two decades, most recently in the 2011 case involving drill pipe and collars from China (Investigation Nos. 701-TA-474 and 731-TA-1176 (Final)).

[53] See, for example, the WTO decision that Boeing received illegal subsidies (Steinhauser 2011).

[54] Note 2, paragraph 1 of Article VI of the GATT reads as follows: "It is recognized that, in the case of imports from a country which has a complete or substantially complete monopoly of its trade and where all domestic prices are fixed by the State, special difficulties may exist in determining price comparability for the purposes of paragraph 1, and in such cases importing contracting parties may find it necessary to take into account the possibility that a strict comparison with domestic prices in such a country may not always be appropriate."

[55] Figure 6 includes exports of all commodities, including oil. However, none of the countries shown in the Figure is a major oil exporter. Furthermore, most exports, especially for these countries, consist of manufactured commodities.

development initiatives. In addition, the U.S. should consider withdrawing from the government procurement agreement, so that more extensive Buy-American programs can be developed.

- There is great need for enhanced reporting and analysis of data on U.S. FDI in China. BEA data on the operations of US MNCs show that U.S. FDI in China reached $162 billion in 2008, about 16.6% of total FDI in China (Figure 3). Other academic research Table 3 below (Xing 2010) reports that the U.S. share was only 6.4%. In addition, U.S. MNCs are accumulating vast stocks of retained earnings abroad (a total of $1.8 trillion was accumulated between 1999 and 2010 alone—see Figure 5 for flows). This may help explain the discrepancy between the data on the flow of new FDI shown in U.S. balance of payments reports, and changes in the stock of US FDI in China (from reports on the operations of US MNCs)—Figure 4 below. These data show that FDI, as reported in U.S. Balance of Payment Statistics, represents just the financial tip of US FDI abroad. Much greater information is needed on how U.S and other MNCs finance foreign operations. Funding for construction of a new factory in China can flow directly from the home company in the United States, from retained earnings abroad, and from borrowed capital. In one widely reported example, Evergreen Solar recently announced that it was closing a factory to make solar panels in Massachusetts, and moving it to China. Chinese banks offered Evergreen financing for two-thirds of the cost of their new plant at rates "as low as 4.8 percent" with no principal payments or interest payments due until the end of the loan in 2015 (Scott 2011). This example illustrates that more and better data are needed on the financing of US FDI abroad. MNCs obtain great benefits from deferring taxes on these earnings. These companies should be required to provide more data on where those earnings are invested.

- In exchange for the great benefits earned by U.S MNCs, including tax deferral and access to OPIC and EXIM bank financing, US MNCs should be required to provide much more data on their domestic and foreign operations. In order to better track trends in outsourcing, all U.S. multinationals should be required to publicly disclose the location, output and employment of domestic facilities that are closed or substantially downsized, and similar, plant-level information should be provided for all new facilities outsourced abroad, including greenfield investments and investments in existing production facilities. Foreign MNCs operating in the United States also benefit from federal, state and local incentives and access to publicly financed foreign trade and investment guarantees. They should be required to provide similar data in exchange. These provisions should also extend to contract manufacturing, technology licensing and other related forms of outsourcing. Finally, multinational retail corporations such as Walmart, Target and CVS that engage in substantial amounts of international goods trade (buying and selling large volumes of imported manufactured products and other commodities) should also be required to report annually on product sourcing and domestic and foreign employment, at the plant level.

- Funding for collection and analysis of data on the operations of U.S. and foreign multinationals needs to be substantially increased. Policies developed using these data can contribute to improvements in U.S. trade balances, and to increases in domestic manufacturing output, employment and tax revenues. Such investments will reduce government budget deficits.

Analysis: Foreign Direct Investment in China

China was the third largest recipient of FDI in the world in 2009, as shown in **Table 1**, behind only Luxembourg and the United States. Some large recipients of FDI, such as Luxembourg and the United Kingdom are heavily involved in financial intermediation, and recycle large shares of their FDI inflows to ultimate destinations in other countries, including China. China received no recorded FDI prior to 1982. China passed several laws allowing for foreign joint ventures (in 1979) and wholly owned foreign enterprises (in 1986) that first opened China to foreign investors (Xing 2010). At first, China granted foreign investors participation in special economic zones (SEZs) and gradually opened all of China to FDI in the late 1990s. However, FDI remains concentrated in China's Southern and Central coastal provinces (Du, Harrison and Jefferson 2011).

Inflows of FDI to China rose rapidly in the early 1990s, plateaued at around $40 billion per year and then took off rapidly following China's entry into the WTO in 2001, as shown in **Figure 1**. FDI in China peaked at $147 billion in 2008, fell sharply during the great recession in 2009 and then increased $27.5 billion (35.2%) in 2010 (Invest in China 2011). Aggregate inflows to China total $1.05 trillion between 1978 and 2010, as shown in **Table 2**, and China is the largest recipient of FDI of all developing countries.

According to reported data, the major sources of FDI in China have been its closest neighbors, as shown in **Table 3**. Hong Kong, Taiwan and Macau (not shown), or greater China, is responsible for about half of the accumulated FDI in China, according to published reports. However, a large share of this investment may be "round-trip," having originated in China and then re-invested there. Such investments are encouraged by the low tax rates and other benefits conferred on foreign investors in China. Prior to 2008, profits of foreign investors were taxed at a 15% rate, while domestic investors faced a statutory income tax rate of 33% (Du, Harrison and Jefferson 2011). This incentive was eliminated, and corporate tax rates were unified at 25% in 2008. However, foreign investors were "grandfathered" in and will continue to receive preferential tax rates until 2012.

The United States and other western nations are reportedly responsible for small shares of FDI in China, as shown in Table 3. However, published academic research and data reviewed below suggests that MNCs from the United States may be under-reporting FDI in China.

Foreign Invested Enterprises (both joint ventures and wholly owned subsidiaries) were responsible for 55% of China's exports and 68% of its trade surplus in 2010, as shown in **Table 4**. Foreign Invested Enterprises (FIEs) employed 3% of China's labor force, but generated about 22% of its output (Whaley and Xin 2010). Their overall productivity was nine times greater than that of the average Chinese firm. Within manufacturing, the productivity ratio of FIEs and domestic firms was 4:1. Due to their high productivity, it is also estimated that FIEs were responsible for about 40% of China's recent economic growth.

Du, Harrison and Jefferson (2011) (DHJ) analyzed a unique dataset on the performance of domestic and FIEs in China. They collected data on all firms that generated more than 5 million yuan in output, and also included all state-owned enterprises (SOEs), most of which exceeded this threshold. Their data demonstrate the remarkable breath and impact of FIEs in China. Their dataset (from the Chinese Ministry of Commerce) included complete information on the performance of 1.5 million enterprises for the period 1998-2007. The number of FIES rose from 96,135 in 1998 to 255,042 in 2007. Enterprises from Hong Kong, Taiwan and Macau (HMT) made up an average of 8.9% of the observations in the dataset over the entire period of investigation. Investors from other countries (largely members of the Organization for Economic Cooperation and Development) represented 7.9% of the observations.

DHJ also evaluated the comparative impacts of FDI from the HMT region with that from other countries. They found that FDI from the HMT countries is not associated with higher productivity at the firm level, while FDI from other countries (primarily those in the OECD) is associated with higher productivity. One explanation for this is that the HMT investments originate in China and embody Chinese technology and management techniques. FDI from firms in the OECD transfers technology and western management systems to Chinese firms. DHJ also found substantial upstream and downstream spillover effects from were associated with investments from other (non HMT) countries.

On average, capital invested in these firms increased 10.7% per year, while labor grew only 1.3%. Total Factor Productivity (TFP) increased 5.6% per year. Real output of these firms grew 13.5% per year, and TFP growth was responsible for a remarkable 40% of that output growth. Overall, estimates are that without FDI, China's GDP growth, which has exceeded 10% per year since 1982 (World Economic Outlook 2011), could have been 3.4% lower (Xing 2010).

FDI plays an even more important role in China's high-tech exports. For example, in the information and computer technology sector, in 1998, China generated $20.3 billion worth of exports in this sector (11% of China's total exports), and FIEs were responsible for 73.7% of this output. In 2008, China exports in this sector increased to $415.6 billion (29.1% of total Chinese exports), and FIEs were responsible for 85.2% of this output.

Reasons for Growth of FDI in China

A number of factors have contributed to the growth of FDI in China. The existence of a large pool of low wage labor has certainly been important, but that labor was not mobilized for the production of exports until China made the decision to become a market economy in the with its "open door" policy and economic reforms of 1978, and reforms of its foreign investment laws in the 1980s noted above (Xing 2010). China has also used a number of activist policies to attract and retain FDI, and to maximize exports and other benefits received from these facilities. First, the RMB (yuan) was devalued by 57.2% between July of 1986 and January of 1994, primarily in three distinct moves (**Figure 2**), and held at this level until July 2005. The best estimates are that the RMB is still 25% to 40% undervalued (Cline 2009 and 2010). China's currency manipulation is illegal under the GATT/WTO agreements and the IMF charter, as well as U.S. law (Scott and Bivens 2006). Currency manipulation dramatically lowers Chinese production costs and provides an effective subsidy to Chinese exports; it also acts as a barrier to imports from other countries. Second, China provided tax holidays and has offered FIEs preferential tax rates for corporate profits (as noted above), and reduced value added tax rates. China has also offered other incentives to MNEs that established subsidiaries and joint ventures in its "Special Economic Zones" (Xing 2010). Finally, China has provided tens of billions of dollars of illegal subsidies to firms in industries such as steel, glass, paper and new green technology industries (Haley 2008, 2009, 2010 and Scott, 2010a and 2011). Most of these incentives and subsidies are illegal under the terms of the WTO and U.S. fair trade laws.

Taken as a whole, China's FDI promotion regime has provided massive, illegal subsidies to MNEs from the United States and other countries. These subsidies have encouraged firms to outsource production from the United States and other developed countries to China; they have contributed to the rapid growth of China's exports to the U.S. and the world; and they have severely suppressed U.S. exports to China, and to the world (China is now the most important competitor for U.S. exports on world markets).

U.S. Outward Foreign Direct Investment

There is great need for enhanced reporting and analysis of data on U.S. FDI in China. BEA data on the operations of US MNCs shows that U.S. FDI in China reached $162 billion in 2008, as shown in **Figure 3**, about 16.6% of total cumulative FDI in China (Table 2, above).[56] Other academic reports Table 3 (Xing 2010) report that the U.S. share was only 6.4%. Data from surveys of the operations of U.S. MNCs in China yield different estimates of the flow of funds to such operations.

Similar results are obtained for the annual flows of U.S. FDI to China. **Figure 4** reports two contrasting estimates. The first is based on data from the U.S. balance of payments statistics (which report on U.S. current and capital account transactions, on a quarterly basis). The second estimate is net change in the value of U.S. FDI in China from the operating statistics reported by U.S. multinational companies (also reported by the BEA), for the period

---

[56] Note that this estimate is conservative. Data on the operations of U.S. MNCs is released about 21 months after the end of a given calendar year. This estimate (16.8%) compares total U.S. FDI in China in 2008 (as reported by US MNCs) with total FDI in China in 2010. It is likely that total U.S. FDI in China, as will be reported by US MNCs, increased in 2009 and 2010 (global inflows of FDI to China slowed in 2009, but they were not reversed; and US BOP data show FDI in China outflows of $7 billion in 2009 more than offset by FDI inflows of $9 billion in 2010, as shown in Figure 4).

1999-2008. There are important conceptual differences in the two series—the latter includes valuation changes while the former does not. But the differences in the data are strikingly large. Flows based on the MNC survey report exceed those in the Balance of Payments statistics by a factor ranging from 2:1 to more than 5:1 for the period covered in Figure 4.

In addition, U.S. MNCs are accumulating vast stocks of retained earnings abroad (a total of $1.8 trillion was accumulated between 1999 and 2010 alone—see **Figure 5** for flows). This may help explain the discrepancy between the data on the flow of new FDI shown in U.S. balance of payments reports, and changes in the stock of US FDI in China (from reports on the operations of US MNCs)—Figure 4. These data show that FDI, as reported in U.S. Balance of Payment Statistics represents just the financial tip of US FDI abroad. Much greater information is needed on how U.S and other MNCs finance foreign operations. Funding for construction of a new factory in China can flow directly from the home company in the United States, from retained earnings abroad, and from borrowed capital. In one widely reported example, Evergreen Solar recently announced that it was closing a factory making solar panels in Massachusetts, and moving it to China. Chinese banks offered Evergreen financing for two-thirds of the cost of their new plant at rates "as low as 4.8 percent" with no principal payments or interest payments due on the loan until the end of 2015 (Scott 2011). This example illustrates that more and better data is needed on the financing of US FDI abroad. MNCs obtain great benefits from deferring taxes on these earnings. These companies should be required to provide more data on where those earnings are invested.

US multinational companies prosper while manufacturing suffers at home

Outsourcing has resulted in the loss of millions of and the closure of tens of thousands of factories in the United States in the past decade, but profits of U.S. multinationals have soared. The U.S. lost 3.6 million manufacturing jobs between January 2000 and December 2007, the peak of the last business cycle, and outsourcing was responsible for the vast majority of these job losses. An additional 2 million manufacturing jobs were lost through February 2011, primarily due to the Great Recession.[57]

The global earnings of U.S. MNCs on direct investment abroad rose from $146 billion in 2000 to $420 billion in 2010, and increase of 187% (earnings are shown on the black line in Figure 5, and measured on the left axis). U.S. MNCs obtain a tremendous financial advantage through FDI because they are allowed to defer taxation on earnings that are not repatriated (that is, those that are reinvested abroad). Figure 5 shows that the share of earnings repatriated (shown on the red bars and measured on the right axis) has fallen from 49% in 1999 to 25% in 2010, while the share repatriated has risen from 51% in 1999 to 75% in 2010 (shown on the blue bars).
The only exception to the trend of a rising share of retained earnings came in 2005, when a special tax incentive was offered to businesses that repatriated earnings. Even in that year, repatriated earnings exceed total earnings that year by only $10 billion.[58] Over the entire period of 1999-2010, U.S. MNCs accumulated over $1.8 trillion in retained earnings abroad (this figure is net of earnings repatriated in all years, including 2005). This is an incredible pool of tax deferred capital that was available to finance FDI abroad in all countries, including China. In effect U.S. taxpayers have subsidized FDI abroad, effectively "loaning" U.S. MNCS approximately $640 billion for FDI abroad.[59] US MNCs are able to invest these funds tax and interest free, and enjoy the profits earned on these investments, until those funds are repatriated to the United States. Based on the trends show in Figure 5, and absent significant changes in U.S. tax and regulatory policy, it is unlikely that the vast majority of those funds will ever be repatriated. They have become, in effect, a permanent subsidy to U.S. MNCs investing abroad.

---

[57] U.S. Bureau of Labor Statistics. 2011. "Current Employment Statistics." http://www.bls.gov/ces/

[58] It is important to note that the 2005 incentives for repatriation of foreign earnings had no discernable effect on total U.S. non-residential investment. The total contribution of fixed non-residential investment to U.S. GDP growth increased from 0.61 percentage points in 2004 to 0.69 points in 2005 to 0.84 points in 2006 before slowing as the U.S. entered the great recession. This pattern is typical for the late stages of a recovery, as businesses begin to bump up against capacity limits. A much stronger upswing in non-residential investment occurred in 1997 and 1998, towards the end of the previous business cycle.

[59] This estimate applies the statutory 35% corporate tax rate to the sum of total retained earnings from FDI abroad for the period 1999-2010.

Conclusions and policy recommendations

The United States can and should adopt new policies to level the playing field between the U.S. and China. Trade and manufacturing policies should be used to defend and recover production in the United States, and to maximize production and employment in U.S. manufacturing establishments. These policies should emphasize the benefits of U.S. production and employment. Support for the headquarters operations of domestic or foreign MNEs should be, at most, a secondary concern of domestic trade policies.

Enforcement of important U.S. fair trade laws, such as anti-dumping and countervailing duty (CVD) measures requires a qualifying group representing domestic producers or workers that generate at least 25% of domestic volume of the like product to file a legal complaint. Litigation of these cases can cost millions of dollars, with uncertain outcomes—many such cases are rejected. As U.S. industries have offshored production, and become increasingly dependent on low-cost foreign suppliers, their interest in filing fair trade complaints has declined. U.S. firms investing in China such as GM, Motorola, Johnson & Johnson, and the Blackstone Group, and large retailers such as Walmart, Target and CVS benefit directly or indirectly from China's currency manipulation and subsidies. These firms are more likely to threaten or otherwise discourage their suppliers from participating in fair-trade enforcement cases. Thus, fewer and fewer trade cases are being filed, simply because of the costs and difficulty of obtaining the support of a qualifying domestic injured party.

Other specific trade and economic development policies that should be considered include:

- Policies that threaten to impose strong sanctions on China for its illegal currency manipulation such as the Fair Trade Act of 2011, co-sponsored by Senators Brown and Snowe and Representatives Ryan and Murphy, and the much tougher Schumer-Graham currency reform measure adopted by the Senate in 2005.
- The Congress should re-authorize the Super 301 provisions in U.S. Trade Law, which required the USTR to initiate negotiations with priority countries to eliminate trade practices that impeded U.S. exports, including currency manipulation.
- The U.S. should establish an independent agency to pursue violations of U.S. unfair trade law, including illegal tax subsidies and other types of direct and indirect subsidies.
- Congress could consider chartering and funding an independent organization, like the Congressional Budget Office that could investigate and file unfair trade complaints on behalf of Congress, or could refer complaints to committee for consideration of Congressional action.
- Recently, a WTO appellate body ruled that U.S. cannot simultaneously apply antidumping and CVDs to products imported from China under its non-market economy rules when imposition of such duties would amount to double-counting, that is, when the prohibited subsidy has contributed to the below-market pricing that is the subject of the anti-dumping margin. This ruling also sharply limited the definition of a "Public Body" (which can deliver subsidies), and rejected claims that State Owned Enterprises (SOEs) "exercised governmental functions on behalf of the Chinese Government." This ruling will sharply limit the ability of the United States to impose Countervailing Duties in cases involving Chinese subsidies. U.S. fair trade law may have to be amended to provide new legal and economic approaches to the assessment of countervailable subsidies that do not affect subject-import prices, and to address the role of SOEs. As an alternative the United States may wish to rethink its commitment to and participation in the WTO dispute settlement mechanism. The U.S. has lost several high-profile cases in recent years and there is a growing perception that WTO appellate judges are choosing "to substitute their own views for the rules negotiated by the WTO parties" (Otteman 2011). The costs of participation in the WTO dispute

resolution process may have begun to exceed its benefits and it may be time for the U.S. to withdraw from the dispute settlement process.

- Rules contained in the 2001 US-China WTO accession agreement regarding treatment of China as a non-market economy (NME) will expire at the end of 2016. Rules governing application of the NME status will then revert to the much tougher WTO standard.[60] Domestic petitioners will be required to prove that "all domestic prices are fixed by the State." China is a mixed economy and manages many, but not all, domestic prices in most cases. The WTO NME rules are clearly defective in this case, and should be revised to allow treatment of China as a NME. If WTO members fail to approve these changes, this will provide another reason why the United States should consider withdrawing from the WTO dispute settlement process.

- U.S. manufacturing is falling further and further behind; China became the largest exporter in the world in 2009 (Figure 6), and recently passed the United States to become the largest manufacturer in the world. One reason for this is that the United States lags far behind other countries in the use of industrial policies and other types of economic development initiatives, such as workforce development and training, publicly supported R&D, and also the use of preferential public procurement policies. China, in particular, is not a signatory to the WTO government procurement agreement. Other OECD countries who are signatories still manage to use government procurement to support domestic industrial development, for example through military offset programs (Herrnstadt 2010). The U.S. needs to develop a wide range of economic development initiatives. In addition, the U.S. should consider withdrawing from the government procurement agreement, so that more extensive Buy-American programs can be developed.

- Funding for collection and analysis of data on the operations of U.S. and foreign multinationals needs to be substantially increased. Policies developed using these data can contribute to improvements in U.S. trade balances, and to increases in domestic manufacturing output, employment and tax revenues. Such investments will reduce government budget deficits.

Table 1: 2009 Foreign Direct Investment, Inflows

---

[60] Note 2, paragraph 1 of Article VI of the GATT reads as follows: "It is recognized that, in the case of imports from a country which has a complete or substantially complete monopoly of its trade and where all domestic prices are fixed by the State, special difficulties may exist in determining price comparability for the purposes of paragraph 1, and in such cases importing contracting parties may find it necessary to take into account the possibility that a strict comparison with domestic prices in such a country may not always be appropriate."

Top Five, Globally

		$ Billions	% of 2009 Total
1	Luxembourg	194.8	17.0%
2	United States	134.7	11.7%
3	China, P.R.: Mainland	78.2	6.8%
4	United Kingdom	72.9	6.4%
5	France	60.0	5.2%

Top 10 Developing

		$ Billions	% of 2009 Total
1	China, P.R.: Mainland	78.2	6.8%
2	China, P.R.: Hong Kong	52.4	4.6%
3	Russian Federation	36.8	3.2%
4	India	34.6	3.0%
5	Brazil	25.9	2.3%
6	Mexico	14.5	1.3%
7	Poland	13.8	1.2%
8	Kazakhstan	13.6	1.2%
9	Chile	12.7	1.1%
10	Turkey	8.4	0.7%

Euro Area

	$ Billions	% of 2009 Total
Euro Area	298.654	26.0%

Source: 2009 FDI Inflows, Dir. Inv. In Rep. Econ., N.I.E., IMF, and Economic Policy Institute.

Table 2: Aggregate FDI Inflows, 1978-2009

Top Five, Globally

		$ Billions	% of World Total
1	United States	3124.1	18.1%
2	United Kingdom	1451.6	8.4%
3	China, P.R.: Mainland	1053.4	6.1%
4	Luxembourg	1021.7	5.9%
5	France	875.2	5.1%

Top 10 Developing Nations

		$ Billions	% of World Total
1	China, P.R.: Mainland	1053.4	6.1%
2	China, P.R.: Hong Kong	427.4	2.5%
3	Brazil	366.2	2.1%
4	Mexico	330.2	1.9%
5	Russian Federation	258.0	1.5%
6	India	168.9	1.0%
7	Saudi Arabia	157.3	0.9%
8	Chile	115.5	0.7%
9	Thailand	101.9	0.6%
10	Turkey	98.3	0.6%

Euro Area

	$ Billions	% of World Total
Euro Area*	2932.461	17.0%

Source: 2009 FDI Inflows, Dir. Inv. In Rep. Econ., N.I.E., IMF, and Economic Policy Institute.
*Note that Euro Area data begins in 1998.

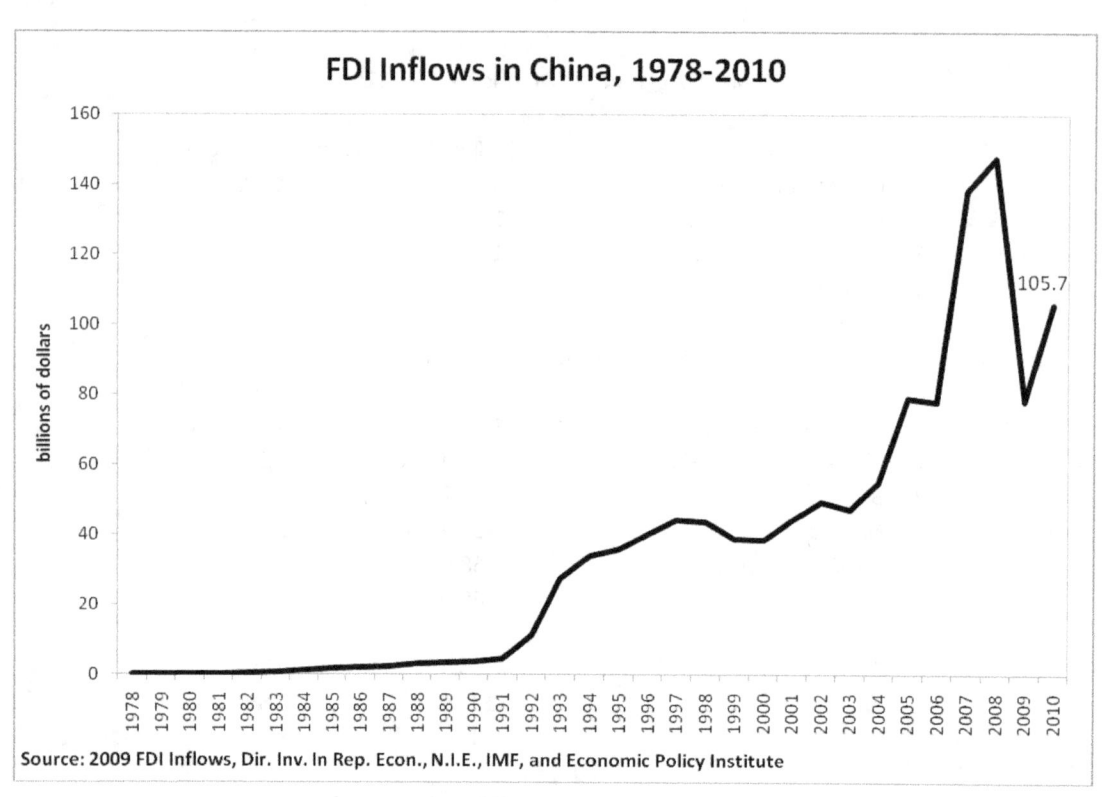

FDI Inflows in China, 1978-2010

Source: 2009 FDI Inflows, Dir. Inv. In Rep. Econ., N.I.E., IMF, and Economic Policy Institute

Table 3: Major Sources of FDI in China, 1985-2008

Major Sources of FDI in China, 1985-2008

Sources	1985-1990 Value (Billion USD)	Share (%)	1991-2000 Value (Billion USD)	Share (%)	2001-2008 Value (Billion USD)	Share (%)	1985-2008 Value (Billion USD)	Share (%)
The World	15.9	100.0	327.7	100.0	510.7	100.0	854.3	100.0
Hong Kong	9.7	60.9	159.0	48.5	178.2	34.9	346.9	40.6
Taiwan	0.0	0.0	25.8	7.9	21.4	4.2	47.2	5.5
Japan	2.2	13.6	25.2	7.7	37.4	7.3	64.7	7.6
Korea	0.0	0.0	10.5	3.2	31.5	6.2	42.0	4.9
Singapore	0.2	1.3	16.8	5.1	20.6	4.0	37.6	4.4
USA	1.9	12.1	27.6	8.4	29.5	5.8	55.1	6.4
Germany	0.2	1.3	6.1	1.9	9.2	1.8	15.5	1.8
UK	0.2	1.2	8.4	2.6	6.9	1.4	15.5	1.8
France	0.1	0.9	4.0	1.2	4.4	0.9	8.6	1.0

Source: table from: Yuqing Xing, "Facts About and Impacts of FDI on China and the World Economy," China, an International Journal, Volume 8, Number 2, September 2010; Table 1, page 7, Economic Policy Institute.

Table 4: China's World Trade, Total, and by Foreign Invested Enterprises, 2009-2010

China's world trade, total and by FIE, billions of USD

	2009	2010	Growth
Exports	1,201.8	1,577.9	31.3%
Imports	1,005.6	1,394.8	38.7%
Trade Balance	196.1	183.1	-6.6%
trade of FIEs	2009	2010	Growth
Exports	672.2	862.3	28.3%
Imports	545.2	738	35.4%
Trade Balance	127.0	124.3	-2.1%
FIE shares of total China trade	2009	2010	Growth
Exports	56%	55%	-2.3%
Imports	54%	53%	-2.4%
Trade Balance	65%	68%	4.8%

Source: China, Ministry of Commerce, PRC,
http://english.mofcom.gov.cn/aarticle/statistic/BriefStatistics/201101/20110107386812.html; Invest in China, PRC,
http://www.fdi.gov.cn/pub/FDI_EN/default.html; Economic Policy Institute.

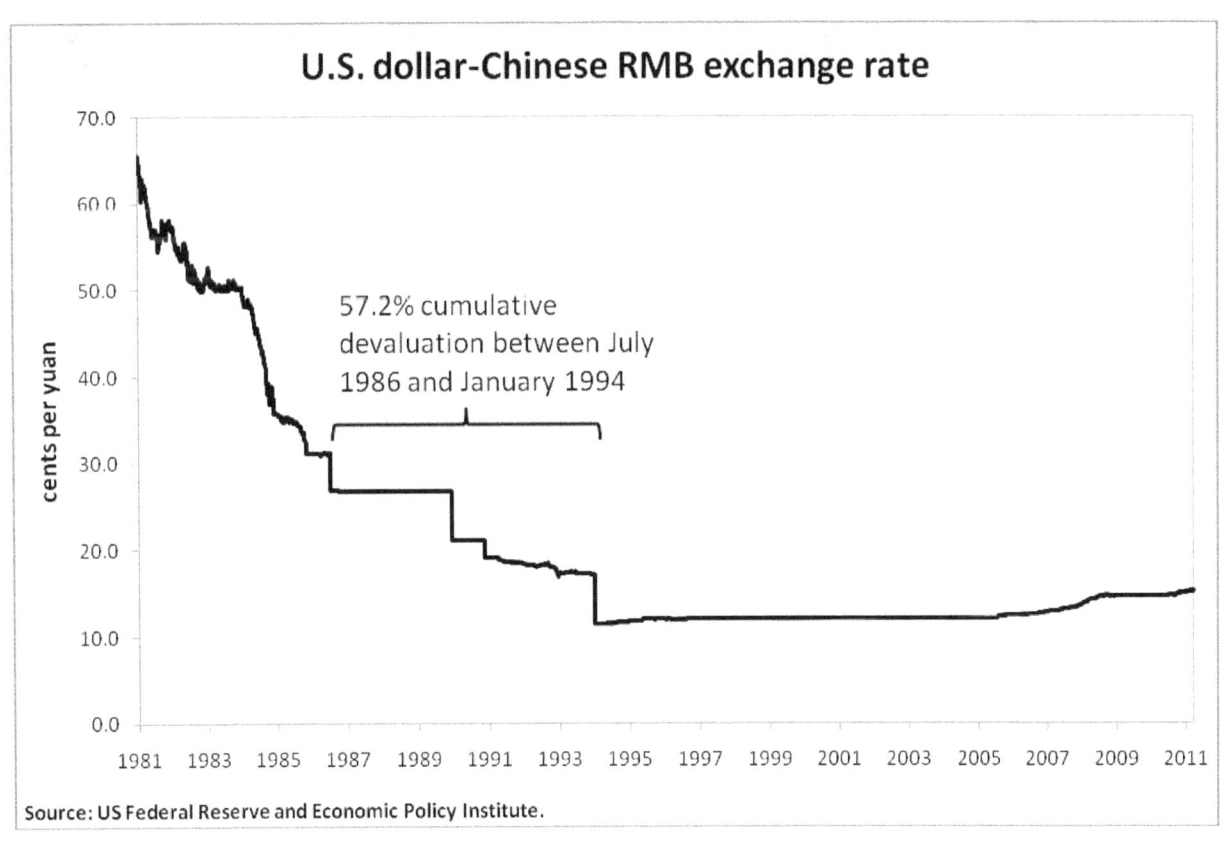

Source: US Federal Reserve and Economic Policy Institute.

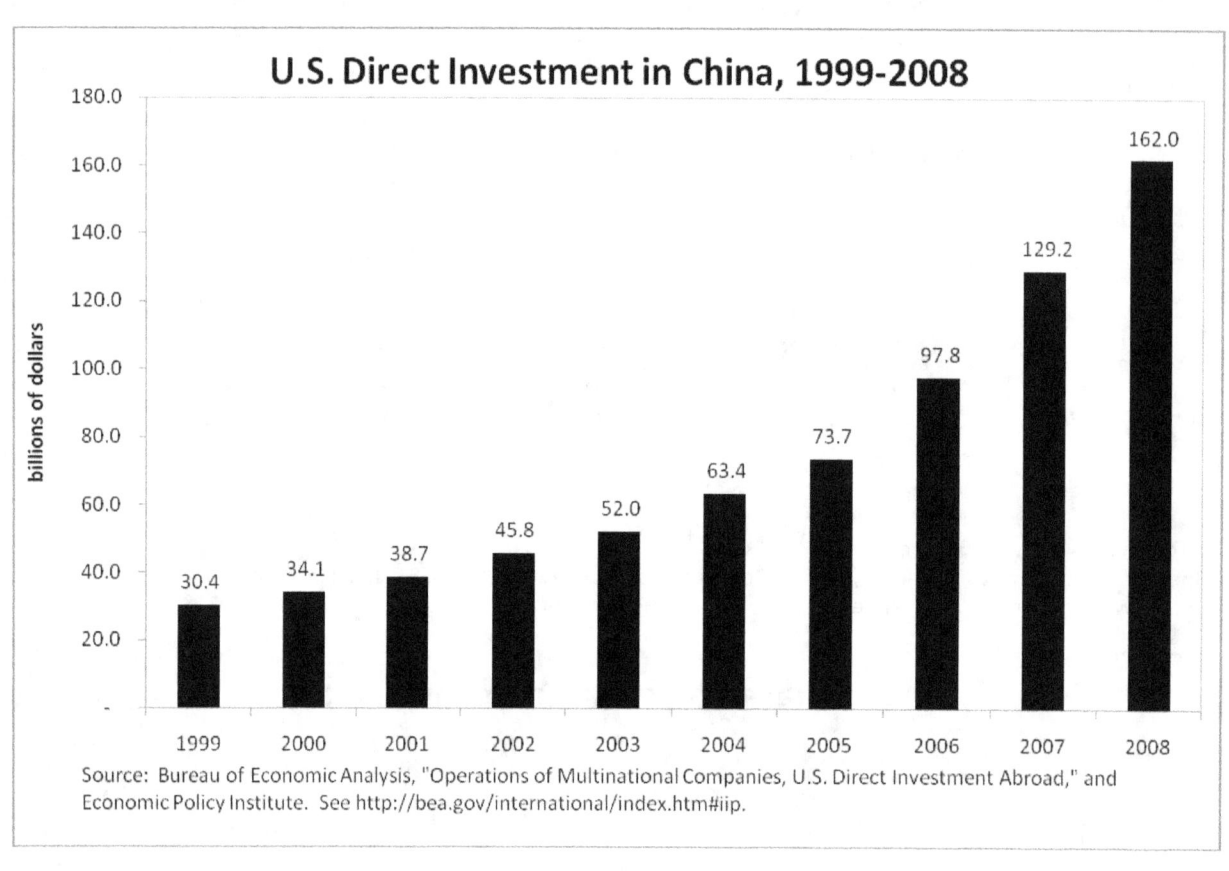

U.S. Direct Investment in China, 1999-2008

Source: Bureau of Economic Analysis, "Operations of Multinational Companies, U.S. Direct Investment Abroad," and Economic Policy Institute. See http://bea.gov/international/index.htm#iip.

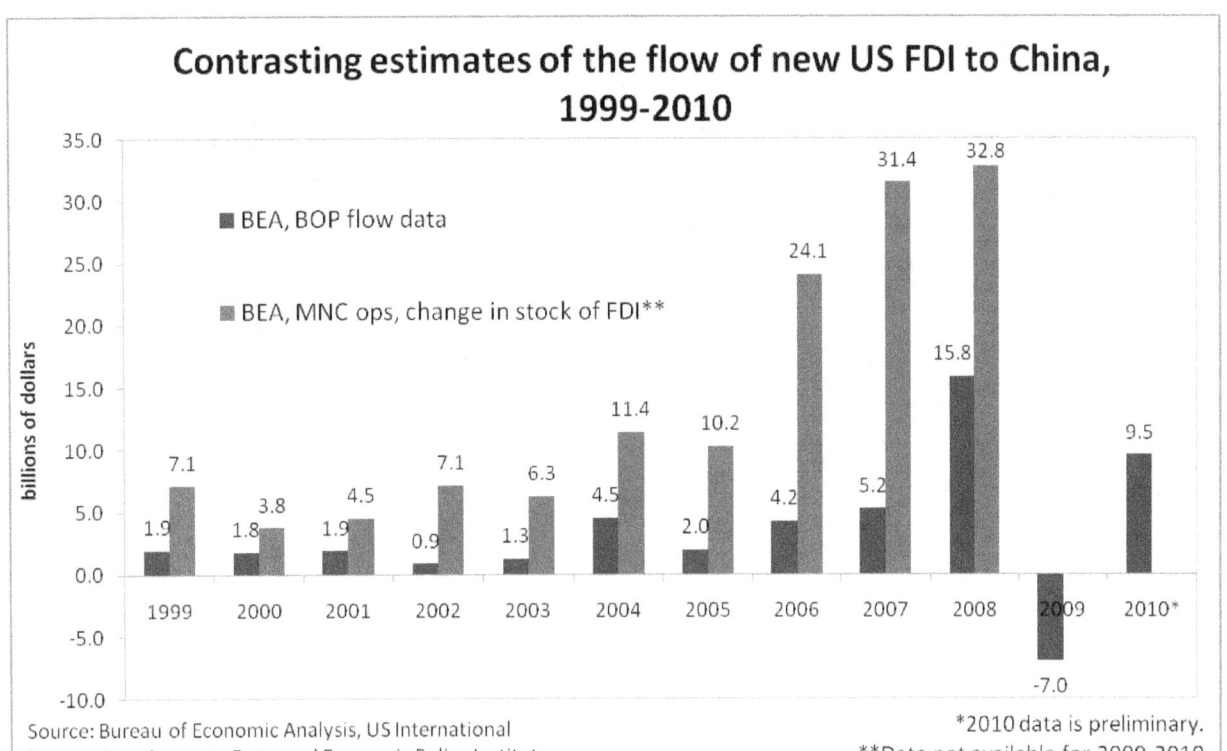

Contrasting estimates of the flow of new US FDI to China, 1999-2010

■ BEA, BOP flow data

■ BEA, MNC ops, change in stock of FDI**

Year	BEA, BOP flow data	BEA, MNC ops
1999	1.9	7.1
2000	1.8	3.8
2001	1.9	4.5
2002	0.9	7.1
2003	1.3	6.3
2004	4.5	11.4
2005	2.0	10.2
2006	4.2	24.1
2007	5.2	31.4
2008	15.8	32.8
2009	-7.0	
2010*	9.5	

Source: Bureau of Economic Analysis, US International Transactions Accounts Data, and Economic Policy Institute.

*2010 data is preliminary.
**Data not available for 2009-2010

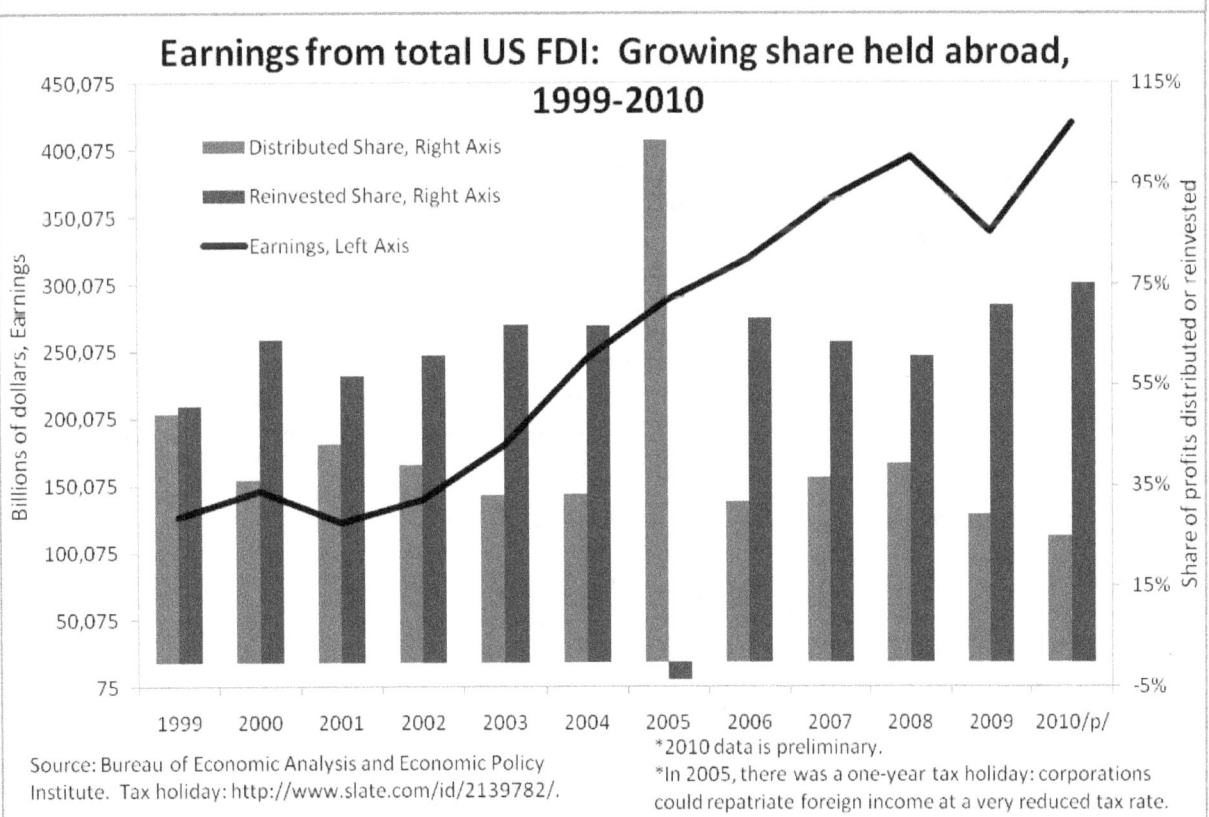

Earnings from total US FDI: Growing share held abroad, 1999-2010

Distributed Share, Right Axis

Reinvested Share, Right Axis

Earnings, Left Axis

Source: Bureau of Economic Analysis and Economic Policy Institute. Tax holiday: http://www.slate.com/id/2139782/.

*2010 data is preliminary.
*In 2005, there was a one-year tax holiday: corporations could repatriate foreign income at a very reduced tax rate.

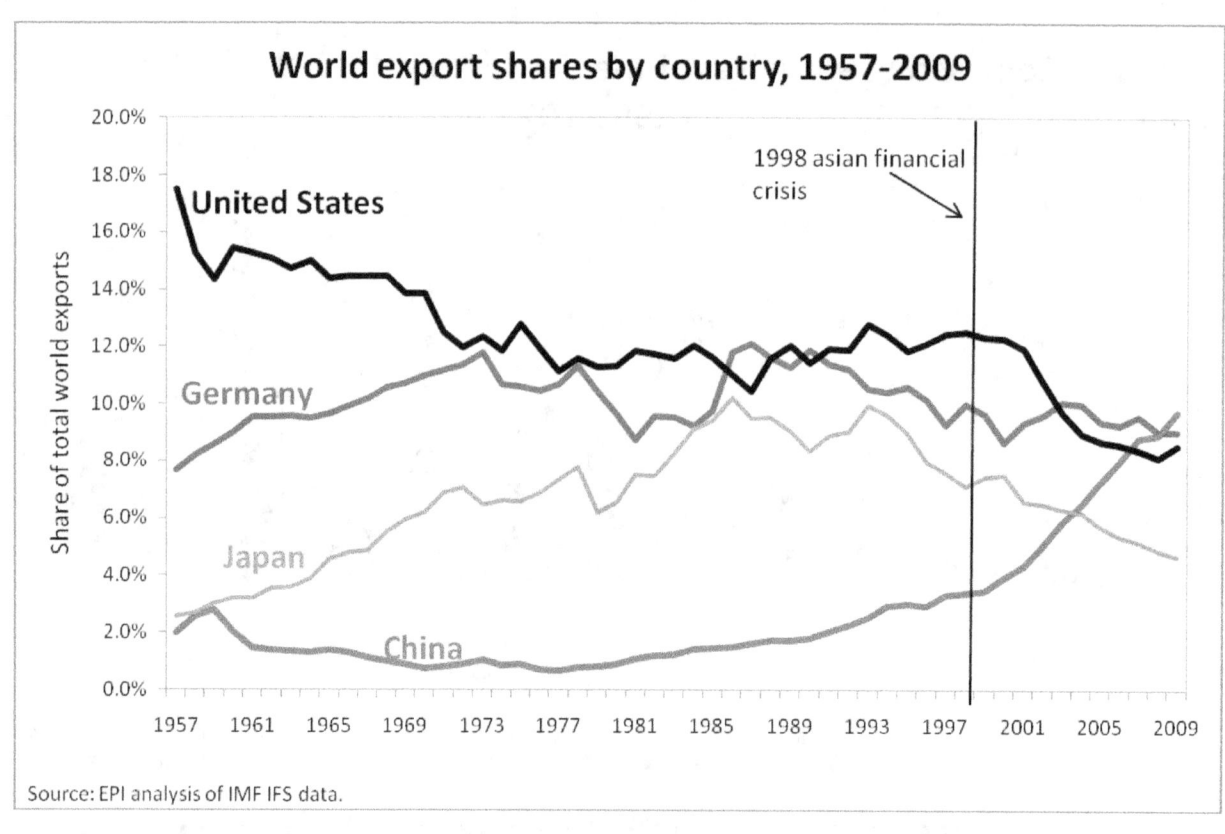

World export shares by country, 1957-2009

1998 asian financial crisis

- United States
- Germany
- Japan
- China

Share of total world exports

Source: EPI analysis of IMF IFS data.

References

Bivens, L. Josh, and Robert Scott. 2006. "China Manipulates Its Currency—A Response is Needed." EPI Policy Memorandum No. 116. Washington, D.C.: Economic Policy Institute. http://www.epi.org/publications/entry/pm116/.

Cline, William, and John Williamson. 2010. "Estimates of Fundamental Equilibrium Exchange Rates." PIIE Policy Brief No. PB10-15. Washington, D.C.: Peterson Institute for International Economics. http://iie.com/publications/interstitial.cfm?ResearchID=1596.

Davies, Ken. 2011. "While global FDI falls, China's outward FDI doubles." Vale Columbia Center on Sustainable International Investment. *Inward and Outward FDI Country Profiles*. Chapter 16, January 2011.

Du, Luosha, Ann Harrison and Gary Jefferson. 2011. "Do Institutions Mater for FDI Spillovers? The Implications of China's Special Characteristics." Cambridge, MA: National Bureau of Economic Research. Working Paper 16767. http://www.nber.org/papers/w16767.

Haley, Usha C.V. 2010. "No Paper Tiger." EPI Briefing Paper No. 264. Washington, D.C.: Economic Policy Institute. http://www.epi.org/publications/entry/no_paper_tiger/.

Haley, Usha C.V. 2008. "Shedding Light on Energy Subsidies in China: An Analysis of China's Steel Industry from 2000-2007." Washington, D.C.: The Alliance for American Manufacturing. http://americanmanufacturing.org/content/shedding-light-energy-subsidies-china-analysis-china%E2%80%99s-steel-industry-2000-2007.

Haley, Usha C.V. 2009. "Through China's looking glass – Subsidies to the Chinese glass industry from 2004-2008." EPI Briefing Paper No. 242. Washington, D.C.: Economic Policy Institute. http://www.epi.org/publications/entry/bp242/.

Invest in China Website. 2011. "Invest in China." Beijing, Ministry of Commerce of the People's Republic of China. http://www.fdi.gov.cn/pub/FDI_EN/default.htm.

Herrnstadt, Owen E. 2008. "Offsets and the lack of a comprehensive U.S. policy: What do other countries know that we don't?" EPI Briefing Paper No. 201. Washington, D.C.: Economic Policy Institute. http://www.epi.org/publications/entry/bp201/.

Ministry of Commerce People's Republic of China Website. 2011. "Ministry of Commerce." Beijing, Ministry of Commerce of the People's Republic of China. http://english.mofcom.gov.cn/statistic/statistic.html.

Otteman, Scott. 2011. "Appellate body reversal on 'double remedies' sparks angry U.S. reaction." Inside China US-Trade, Vol. 11, No. 11, March 16 2011.

Scott, Robert. 2011. "Can the US compete with China on Green Tech? Ways to Recapture the Lead." Room for Debate. New York, New York: The New York Times. http://www.nytimes.com/roomfordebate/2011/01/18/can-the-us-compete-with-china-on-green-tech/ways-for-the-us-can-recapture-the-lead.

Scott, Robert. 2010a. "China's Subsidies to Green Industries Lead to Growing Trade Deficits in Clean Energy Products." EPI Press Release. Washington, D.C.: Economic Policy Institute. http://www.epi.org/publications/entry/ib287/.

Scott, Robert. 2010b. "Unfair China Trade Costs Local Jobs." EPI Briefing Paper No. 260. Washington, D.C.: Economic Policy Institute. http://www.epi.org/publications/entry/bp260/.

Steinhauser, Gabrielle. 2011. "WTO finds Boeing got illegal subsidies." Komo News. http://www.komonews.com/news/boeing/114932729.html.

Whalley, John and Xian Xin. 2010. "China's FDI and non-FDI economies and the sustainability of future high Chinese growth." China Economic Review, volume 21, 2010, pp. 123-135.

Xing, Yuqing. 2010. "Facts About and Impacts of FDI on China and the World Economy." China: an International Journal, Volume 8, Number 2, September 2010, pp. 309-32.

HEARING CO-CHAIR WESSEL: Thank you.
Dr. Fung.

STATEMENT OF DR. K.C. FUNG, PROFESSOR OF ECONOMICS, UNIVERSITY OF CALIFORNIA, SANTA CRUZ, CALIFORNIA

DR. FUNG: Thank you so much for allowing me to be here. I just want to focus on the topic of foreign and U.S. investment in China. As Dr. Moran and Dr. Scott mentioned and highlighted, China continues to be an extremely attractive destination for foreign direct investors. In 2010, the amount of FDI in China amounted to more than $105 billion. That's up from 90 billion.

DR. SCOTT: Trillion, "t", trillion.

DR. FUNG: It's flows.

DR. SCOTT: Oh, flows. Pardon me.

DR. FUNG: Not the stock. But, yes, if you add up all the years, it's in trillions. So the most popular mode of FDI, as we know, takes the form of wholly foreign-owned enterprises. One reason is it reflects the increasing knowledge of American and foreign companies in understanding the labor and the consumer markets in China. Secondly, until 2008, there seemed to be some zigzag, but the trend was increasing openness for foreign direct investors.

However, as the first panel highlighted, due to the indigenous innovation policy, there have been a lot of complaints by foreign firms about the difficulty that they face in the domestic Chinese market.

Unlike other developing countries, China's sources of funds typically come from other Asian economies, particularly Hong Kong and Taiwan. Of course, even for these economies, it's difficult to decipher exactly where some of these funds come from. Potentially, they could even be from mainland China itself.

In 2009, about half, a little more than half of the inflows into China came, according to official statistics, from Hong Kong, and the U.S. came in seventh. It represents only about 2.8 percent of total inflows into China. In terms of stocks, that's similar. Hong Kong, again, is the largest direct investor, with the U.S. coming in fourth.

As we all know now, a lot of the statistics increasingly show the tax haven economies like Virgin Islands, Cayman Islands have become more and more important sources of FDI so that makes it even more difficult to understand where the true sources of funds are really coming from.

A popular interpretation among some researchers are that these funds that come from Virgin Islands and Cayman Islands also originally would come from Hong Kong, Taiwan and mainland China, even though it's difficult to test exactly whether that is the case.

In terms of outward direct investment, even though we're not talking about outward, but again mainland China invested more or most in Hong Kong as the top destination in 2009. The U.S. was sixth as the most popular destination.

There are some new studies that tend to show that some of these outward direct investments from mainland China, after controlling for motives of resources seeking, they tend to end up in more corrupt economies where corruption is illustrated by indices created by a variety of international organizations.

Suppose we look at it from the U.S. rather than just comparing U.S. position in China. U.S. direct investment in China only represents about less than two percent, about 1.4 percent, of total U.S. direct investment abroad. The top destination for U.S. direct investment would be Netherlands, the UK, Canada, Bermuda, and Luxembourg. Again, these are stocks so it represents all the past investments that U.S. had done.

And the bulk of U.S. investment in China was in manufacturing, and about 12 percent in computer and electronic products, about ten percent in chemicals.

There are some detailed firm level studies recently that show that Hong Kong and Taiwanese firms and other foreign companies, including the U.S. companies, they have significantly higher rates of return on the capital in China compared to state-owned enterprises. Perhaps that's not very surprising given that some of these state-owned enterprises are poorly run and face not the discipline by the marketplace.

According to our own government's publication, Survey of Current Business, our multinationals abroad in all destinations, earn about 9.7

percent return. If you use the same methodology and apply it to China alone, the rate of return in 2009 would be 13.5, which is a little bit higher than the average even though one could interpret that to reflect the higher risk of investment in a developing and transition economy like China.

However, as is already well-known now, the latest AmCham-China reports have shown, on one hand, that a large majority of the member firms surveyed reported that operations were either very profitable or profitable, and about 28 percent of the firms reported that China is the number one priority for global investment.

However, for the very first time, U.S. companies reported inconsistent regulatory interpretation as the number one business challenge in China, replacing management level human resource constraints which have been the traditional reason for challenges in China.

Less than three percent of European Union FDI went to China in 2008. Again, according to their own European Union Chamber Business Confidence Survey, 36 percent of the firms said that the regulatory environment has become less fair towards foreign-invested enterprises in the last two years, and slightly more than 36 percent also predicted that the future trend would be increasingly worse for the European firms in China.

So lastly, what are the roles for FDI and U.S. investment in China? One, obviously, the FDI increase GDP in China. According to our own government's estimate, again, Bureau of Economic Analysis estimated in 2008, .6 percent of the Chinese GDP was increased due to our investment there.

Some independent studies also show that our own investment in China contributed more to China's growth in output compared to other sources of FDI, including sources from Hong Kong, Japan, Taiwan or South Korea.

Second role is obviously well-known--the close linkage between FDI and trade. More than half of the imports and exports of trade associated with China are conducted by foreign direct, foreign firms located in China.

Again, as highlighted by Dr. Moran, partly because of the investment from the U.S. and other countries, that facilitated the global supply chain. About 32 percent of the imported intermediate goods were incorporated in Chinese exports, and they mostly come from the four Asian tigers as well as from Japan.

And lastly, that according to our own figures, that our non-bank affiliates in China employed about 950,000 employees in China, and they also spend $1.5 billion in research and development in China. That is our own U.S. affiliates located in China.

There is a growing literature, as we are well aware, that these forms of globalization and offshoring, not only to China but also to India, have created substantial economic and job insecurity in the U.S., and there is some preliminary labor market studies that seem to show that there is a semi-hollowing out effect of the medium-skilled jobs in the United States

associated with offshoring and in conjunction with technological change.
Thank you.
[The statement follows:]

PREPARED STATEMENT OF DR. K.C. FUNG, PROFESSOR OF ECONOMICS, UNIVERSITY OF CALIFORNIA, SANTA CRUZ, CALIFORNIA

In this paper, I would like to discuss various characteristics, trends and roles of U.S. and foreign direct investment (FDI) in China. First, we consider FDI and U.S. direct investment, using Chinese official statistics. While it is clear that the quality of U.S. direct investment data is much better than that of the Chinese data, the use of official Chinese data allows us to examine U.S. direct investment in China in a comparative perspective. Then, in the next section, we will utilize U.S. official data as well as surveys from foreign investors' associations to study some characteristics of foreign and U.S. direct investment. Lastly, we will discuss the roles of foreign and U.S. direct investment in China, using U.S. official data and some relevant academic studies.

China continues to be a very attractive destination for foreign direct investors. In 2010, the amount of FDI in China amounted to US$105.7 billion, up from US$90.0 billion in 2009 (Table 1). The most popular mode of FDI takes the form of wholly foreign owned enterprises (Table 2). There may be two reasons that contributed to this trend. First, foreign investors used to lack detailed knowledge of the Chinese labor and consumer markets so that joint ventures with local partners make more business sense. However, over time, foreign investors, including U.S. investors, increasingly are able to operate in China without the need for Chinese partners. Second, at least until recently, the business environment in China has been increasingly open, which permits foreign investors to have more commercial freedom in their choice of modes of operations. The business environment for foreign investors however, may be changing for the worse since the Chinese government announced the consideration of the so-called "indigenous innovation" policy.

In terms of FDI flows and using official Chinese statistics, the largest FDI came from Hong Kong, with US$46.075 billion in 2009 (Table 3). This represents slightly more than half, with 51.2 percent of the total inflows for that year. The United States came in seventh, with US$2.555 billion. This represents only 2.84 percent of total inflows into China. In terms of stocks (not shown in the appendix), Hong Kong again was the largest foreign direct investor in 2008, with US$349.6 billion. The United States came in fourth in 2008, with US$59.65 billion.

In recent years, tax haven economies such as Virgin Islands and Cayman Islands have become more and more prominent as sources of FDI into China. This makes the FDI statistics more difficult to decipher as funds from these tax haven economies originally come from other places. A popular interpretation is that these funds predominantly come from other Asian sources, particularly Taiwan. As a comparison, Table 4 lists the top ten destinations of Chinese investment abroad. Again, Hong Kong was the top destination for Chinese direct investment abroad, with a flow of US$35.6 billion in 2009. The United States was the sixth most popular destination for outward Chinese foreign direct investment for that year.

Using official U.S. statistics, U.S. direct investment position in China amounted to US$49,403 million in 2009. This represents only 1.4 percent of the total U.S. direct investment abroad. In 2009, the top five destinations for U.S. direct investment were Netherlands (13.4%), the United Kingdom (13.4%), Canada (7.4%), Bermuda (7.0%) and Luxembourg (5.0%). The United States invested more in Mexico (2.8%) and in Singapore (2.2%) than in China (Ibarra-Caton 2010). Of the U.S. direct investment in China, the bulk was in manufacturing, with 45.8 percent in 2009. 11.6 percent was in computer and electronic products and 10.1percent was in chemicals.

According to Liu and Siu (2006), Hong Kong/Taiwanese firms and other foreign firms operating in China are estimated to have significantly higher rates of returns on capital compared to state-owned enterprises. According to Survey of Current Business (Bureau of Economic Analysis September 2010), the rate of return on U.S. Direct Investment abroad to all destinations was 9.7%, using the historical-cost method. Using the same method, the rate of return of U.S. direct investment in China can be calculated to be 13.5% in 2009. Thus the rate of return of U.S. direct investment in China tends to be higher than the average rate of return of all U.S. direct investment abroad. According to AmCham-China (2010), in 2009, 71 percent of the member firms surveyed reported that their operations were profitable or very profitable. In addition, 28 percent of the firms reported that China is their number one priority in global investment. In addition, 58 percent of the U.S. companies source and produce for the Chinese domestic market. Only 12 percent of the U.S. firms produce or source goods or services in China for the U.S. market. However, for the first time, U.S. companies reported "inconsistent regulatory interpretation" as the number one business challenge, replacing "management-level human resource constraints", which was the number one business difficulty since 2008.

Only less than 3% of European Union FDI went to China in 2008. However, the European firms operating in China seem to have similar concerns about the trend of the regulatory environment in China. According to the European Union Chamber Business Confidence Survey, 36% of the firms surveyed said that the regulatory environment has become less fair towards foreign-invested enterprises in the last two years (European Union Chamber of Commerce in China 2010/2011).

What roles do FDI and U.S. direct investment play in China? There are several important economic functions. First, FDI and U.S. direct investment in China increase Chinese output. The value added of U.S. non-bank majority-owned affiliates in China was 0.6% of Chinese GDP in 2008 (Barefoot and Mataloni Jr. 2010). According to a study by Chantasasawat, Fung, Ng and Siu (2011), of all the foreign direct investment in China, the U.S. direct investment contributed most to the increase in Chinese output. The U.S. direct investment is estimated to be more potent than investment from Hong Kong, Japan, Taiwan or Republic of Korea.

Second, while much of the focus of U.S. companies in China seems to be on the domestic Chinese market, foreign-invested enterprises (FIEs) in general often act to serve as a part of the production network that ultimately sends the finished products to consumers in the rich economies such as the United States and Europe. Much of the exports from China and imports into China have been conducted by foreign firms (Table 6). According to Naughton (2007), most of the recent largest exporters of high-technology products from China including Tech-Front Shanghai, ASUStek Computer Suzhou and Motorola China have their parent companies in Taiwan or in the United States.
A recent study commissioned by the United States International Trade Commission (Dean, Fung and Wang 2008) concluded that foreign firms in China facilitated the creation of an Asian production network. Almost 32 percent of the imported intermediate goods that were incorporated in Chinese exports came from the four Asian tigers (Hong Kong, Taiwan, Republic of Korea and Singapore). 18.3 percent came from Japan and 10.3 percent came from the rest of East and Southeast Asia.

U.S. direct investment in China and in Asia facilitated the imports and exports of parts and components from one Asian economy to another. According to Fung, Iizaka and Siu (2011), a one percent increase in U.S. direct investment in China or in another Asian economy will increase exports of parts and components to another Asian economy by 0.37 percent.

Because of the production network facilitated by U.S. and other FDI in China and Asia, intra-Asian trade in parts and components has increased over the years. Much of such Asian trade- and FDI-led integration occurred initially without the presence of significant formal trade agreements. This de facto form of integration is quite different in origin compared to other regional groupings such as Latin America (Aminian, Fung and Ng 2008). In fact, East Asia seems to have a deeper degree of integration compared to integration among Latin America economies (Fung, Garcia-Herreo and Siu 2011).

Lastly, U.S. multinationals operating in China also increases employment in China. In 2008, non-bank U.S. affiliates in China employed 950,200 employees in China. On average, these U.S. affiliates paid US$10,908.2 as annual compensations to their employees. The non-bank majority owned U.S. affiliates in China also spent US$1,517 million in research and development expenditures. This compares to US$582 million in India and US$ 1,872 million in Japan.

References:

AmCham-China, 2010, "2010 China Business Climate Survey," Beijing, People's Republic of China.

Aminian, Nathalie, K.C. Fung and Francis Ng, 2008, "Market Integration vs. Agreements between Markets," World Bank Policy Research Paper No. 4546, Trade Team, Development Research Group, March, The World Bank: Washington, D.C.

Barefoot, Kelvin B. and Raymond J. Mataloni, Jr., 2010, "U.S. Multinational Companies: Operations in the United States and Abroad in 2008," August, Survey of Current Business, Bureau of Economic Analysis, U.S. Department of Commerce, U.S. Government, Washington, D.C.

Bureau of Economic Analysis, Survey of Current Business, 2010, "U.S. Direct Investment Tables," September, Department of Commerce, U.S. Government, Washington, D.C.

Chantasasawat, Busakorn, K.C. Fung, Francis Ng, and Alan Siu, 2011, "Domestic Investment, Alternative Sources of Foreign Direct Investment and

Economic Growth in China," in Linda Yueh (ed.), The Future of Asian Trade and Growth: Economic Development with the Emergence of China, World Scientific Publication, forthcoming.

Dean, Judith, K.C. Fung and Zhi Wang, 2008, "How Vertically Specialized is Chinese Trade?" Working Paper No. 2008-09-D, Office of Economics, U.S. International Trade Commission, U.S. Government, Washington, D.C.

Fung, K.C., Alicia Garcia-Herrero and Alan Siu, 2011, "Production Sharing in Latin America and East Asia," in The Rise of Asia and China: What is in it for Latin America?, eds. K.C. Fung and Alicia Garcia-Herrero, Routledge Press, forthcoming.

European Union Chamber of Commerce in China, 2010/2011, "European Business in China Position Paper," Beijing: People's Republic of China.

Ibarra-Caton, Marilyn, 2010, "Direct Investment Positions for 2009: Country and Industry Detail," July, Survey of Current Business, Bureau of Economic Analysis, Department of Commerce, U.S. Government, Washington, D.C.

Fung, K.C., Hitomi Iizaka and Alan Siu, 2011, "U.S., Japanese and Korean FDI and Intra-Regional East Asian Trade," Asian Economic Papers, forthcoming.

Naughton, Barry, 2007, The Chinese Economy: Transitions and Growth, MIT Press, Cambridge: Massachusetts.

Qiao Liu and Alan Siu, 2011, "Institutions, Financial Development, , and Corporate Investment: Evidence on an Implied Return on Capital in China," Journal of Financial and Quantitative Analysis, forthcoming.

Appendix

Table 1. Total FDI in China

($US millions)

Year	Inflow	Inward Stock	Outflow	Outward Stock
2000	40,715	346,637	*916	*27,768
2001	46,878	393,512	*6,885	*34,654
2002	52,743	446,255	2,700	29,900
2003	53,505	501,474	2,855	33,222
2004	60,630	562,104	5,498	44,777
2005	60,325	622,429	12,261	57,206
2006	63,021	691,897	21,160	90,630
2007	74,768	760,218	26,506	117,911
2008	92,395	852,613	55,907	183,971
2009	90,033	942,646	56,528	245,755
2010	105,735			

Sources: China Statistical Yearbook, various issues

Invest in China [www.fdi.gov.cn]
2009 Statistical Bulletin of China's Outward Foreign Direct Investment, China's Ministry of Commerce
*UNCTADstat

Table 2. Modes of FDI

($US millions)

	Equity Joint Venture	Contractual Joint Venture	Wholly Foreign-owned Enterprise	FDI Shareholding Inc.	Joint Exploration	Others
2007	15,596	1,416	57,264	492	0	0
2008	17,318	1,903	72,315	859	0	0
2009	17,273	2,034	68,682	2,044	0	0
2010	22,498	1,616	80,975	646	0	0

Sources: China Statistical Yearbook, various issues
            Invest in China [www.fdi.gov.cn]

Table 3. Top 10 largest FDI investing economies in China (ranked by foreign investment actually utilized)

Year 2007		Year 2008		Year 2009	
Economy	($US mil)	Economy	($US mil)	Economy	($US mil)
Hong Kong	27,703	Hong Kong	41,036	Hong Kong	46,075
Virgin Islands	16,552	Virgin Islands	15,954	Virgin Islands	11,299
Rep. of Korea	3,678	Singapore	4,435	Japan	4,105
Japan	3,589	Japan	3,652	Singapore	3,605
Singapore	3,185	Cayman Islands	3,145	Rep. of Korea	2,700
United States	2,616	Rep. of Korea	3,135	Cayman Islands	2,582
Cayman Islands	2,571	United States	2,944	United States	2,555
Samoa	2,170	Samoa	2,550	Samoa	2,020
Taiwan	1,774	Taiwan	1,899	Taiwan	1,881
Mauritius	1,333	Mauritius	1,494	Germany	1,217

Table 4. Top 10 destinations for China's outward FDI

($US millions)

	Flow (2009)		Stock (2009)	
	Economy	($US mill)	Economy	($US mill)
1	Hong Kong	35,601	Hong Kong	164,499
2	Cayman Islands	5,366	Virgin Islands	15,061
3	Australia	2,436	Cayman Islands	13,577
4	Luxembourg	2,270	Australia	5,863
5	Virgin Islands	1,612	Singapore	4,857
6	Singapore	1,414	United States	3,338
7	United States	909	Luxembourg	2,484
8	Canada	613	South Africa	2,307
9	Macau	456	Russia	2,220
10	Myanmar	377	Macau	1,837

Source: 2009 Statistical Bulletin of China's Outward Foreign Direct Investment, China's Ministry of Commerce

Table 5. U.S. Direct Investment Position in China (Historical-Cost Basis) in millions of dollars

2005	2006	2007	2008	2009
19,016	26,459	29,710	52,521	49,403

Source: Survey of Current Business, Bureau of Economic Analysis, "Table on U.S. Direct Investment Abroad: Selected Items by Detailed Country, 2005-2009", 2010.

Table 6. Exports and Imports conducted by FIEs

($US millions)

	Exports	Imports	Total
2007	695,520	559,408	1,254,928
2008	790,620	619,956	1,410,576
2009	672,230	545,207	1,217,437
2010	862,306	738,001	1,600,307

Sources: Invest in China [www.fdi.gov.cn]

PANEL III: DISCUSSION, QUESTIONS AND ANSWERS

HEARING CO-CHAIR WESSEL: Thank you, gentlemen, and thank you for the thoroughness of your both prepared as well as oral comments. It is deeply appreciated and shows a tremendous amount of work which will certainly assist the Commission.

Dr. Moran, if I could start with some comments that you made, the sort of a good news/bad news approach that you described. You say that 90 percent, as I recall, 96 percent of high-tech exports come from foreign-invested enterprises.

When we look at the job challenge here in the United States and where we both will grow in the future as well, both as an economy overall, but also in terms of job creation, as we continue to face high unemployment, there are a lot of people who see the migration of that ATP base, understanding, as you said, there is still a lot of supplies coming from here, but that that is accelerating in China, that there is an acceleration of our R&D investments by U.S. MNCs with fairly high profile, and large investments by Microsoft, Delphi. GE just signed a joint venture investment, an R&D agreement, in December, as I recall.

What do you see on the horizon as it relates to economic and job creation here vis-a-vis MNCs' activities in China and, please, Dr. Fung and Dr. Scott, your response, as well?

DR. MORAN: I'm carefully maintaining eye contact once again because the answer, I don't see it as a zero sum problem. What you find is that in the ATP sector, for example, I think I put this in my paper--if I don't, I'll give an addendum to it--what you find is we're not trading the same products.

In the example that I give, I believe in my paper, is that in microscopes--

HEARING CO-CHAIR WESSEL: No, no. In--

DR. MORAN: --our exports average ten to $20,000 per microscope. Our imports are on the one to $200 range so--

HEARING CO-CHAIR WESSEL: Understand. No, my question is more about what's happening now with the R&D.

DR. MORAN: Yes.

HEARING CO-CHAIR WESSEL: Is that there are many who believe that R&D and production are closely linked.

DR. MORAN: Yes.

HEARING CO-CHAIR WESSEL: So that if you believe that, the large investments by a number of U.S. MNCs--will that change or skew what you've described? If a Microsoft has a half billion dollar investment enterprise, their R&D enterprise, is that going to change over time the distribution that you're describing in terms of where the wealth is coming from, that the hundred times or whatever--

DR. MORAN: Right, right.

HEARING CO-CHAIR WESSEL: --microscope is no longer going to be here, but ultimately will migrate to China?

DR. MORAN: Yes. It could be. It's very hard to predict that. We don't see much of that yet. This sounds counterintuitive because you see the high profile things like Microsoft that you said, but two-tenths of one percent of the worldwide R&D done by American multinationals is being done in China, two-tenths of one percent, so it's not like one percent. It's not like it's ten percent. It's very, very small.

Now, ten years from now we may see a dramatic increase in that. I can't predict that, and that will reverberate. I would go back to my argument, though, even if Microsoft--I mean even if the American firms start to do a lot more R&D, I think the benefits are going to be other multinationals and other input suppliers in China, not the Chinese firms, partly for the reasons--I point to Derek who is no longer here--but I mean partly because of the distortions and the uncompetitiveness of many of the Chinese firms.

So we're going to see things change, but I'm less anxious about it than some others.

HEARING CO-CHAIR WESSEL: I understand. Dr. Fung? Dr. Scott?

DR. SCOTT: I am concerned about the growth of R&D abroad. I think it is tied to the outsourcing of U.S. manufacturing. Regarding the role of manufacturing in the United States, although the share of employment involved in manufacturing has declined fairly steadily over the past 40 or 50 years and precipitously in the last decade, the share of the GDP contributed by manufacturing shipments has remained relatively constant in this period. It's over a third of the economy.

That's because manufacturing is a huge consumer of research and development and legal services and other kinds of high-value added service and commodity inputs that are embodied in the manufactured goods.

And what's happening is, as we ship manufacturing abroad, is that demand for a lot of those service inputs are going to go abroad as well. I am very worried about this, and a lot of the R&D that you're talking about is purchased from professional and technical service industries. It's sold to manufacturing so we don't see it directly in terms of lost jobs in manufacturing.

HEARING CO-CHAIR WESSEL: Dr. Fung.

DR. FUNG: Yes. For the U.S. national economic welfare, it seems that innovation is our lifeblood, and so this is an area that we definitely need to pay attention to even though the amount or the share is still very, very small, and, of course, the previous session discussed how China is now targeting a lot of these sectors with increased subsidies, and part of these subsidies are also to research and development as well.

So I wonder sometimes, there may be some reasons why a lot of the big multinationals are setting up all these research labs in China, India, because they can pay much lower wages and compensations, therefore, for the brain powers that could be there.

However, if somehow due to poor intellectual property rights environment, even if you sort of own the knowledge that got generated there, whether it got leaked out to other parts of the local economies, that may be an issue as well.

Thank you.

HEARING CO-CHAIR WESSEL: Thank you.

Commissioner Wortzel.

COMMISSIONER WORTZEL: Dr. Scott, you said you'd welcome a couple of questions about your recommendations, and we really appreciate recommendations because they help inform what we do. But I have questions on the two new independent organizations or agencies you recommended be created on page ten of your written testimony.

The first is establish an independent agency to pursue violations of U.S. unfair trade law, including tax subsidies and other types of direct and indirect subsidies. And here, I'll reveal my own ignorance, which is usually pretty easy to do.

[Laughter.]

COMMISSIONER CLEVELAND: Effortless.

[Laughter.]

COMMISSIONER WORTZEL: Why do we need new agencies? What agency should be doing that now, and why do you think they're ineffective?

Second, your next recommendation is that Congress should consider chartering and funding an independent organization like the CBO that could investigate and file unfair trade complaints on behalf of Congress or refer complaints to Congress for action.

First of all, where would Congress file an unfair trade complaint? I mean isn't that an executive branch responsibility? And second, why do we need a new independent agency when Congress already has the Congressional Research Service with a very broad mandate that they could direct to do these things if they so want?

DR. SCOTT: My concern is that in order to file a trade case, one has to assemble a quorum representing 25 percent of the producers, of the workers, in an industry, in order to file a case, and they have to be willing and able to come up with millions of dollars it can take to file such a case. That's a system we've relied on for decades to enforce our fair trade laws.

That system is falling apart as we offshore production, number one, as the number of domestic producers willing and able to file such cases falls.

Number two, many U.S. firms are now invested abroad, and so they are much less interested in filing cases, for example, against subsidies in China. Many U.S. firms benefit directly from those subsidies.

Take the auto companies as a good example. General Motors is there; Ford is there; Chrysler, as well. And they're buying billions of dollars in parts in China, benefiting, I believe, from substantial subsidies. Not only are they not likely to file cases complaining about that, they're likely to tell their suppliers not to file cases about that as well.

So who is going to represent the American interest? That is the question. Right now my understanding is that the only agency in the government that could--well, there are two agencies that could file some charges. The USTR, but the USTR is not interested in enforcing U.S. trade law. They're more interested in giving away U.S. fair trade laws through trade negotiations, I would contend, and they're part of the executive branch. They are part of the White House, and so actions that they might take are often offset against other foreign policy considerations.

So that's why I think it's so important to have an independent agency that can focus on just this issue of enforcement of the fair trade laws. So that's why I make the first recommendation for an independent agency.

Regarding my proposal to create a congressional agency that could investigate and file unfair trade complaints, my understanding--correct me if I'm wrong. I'm not a trade lawyer--is that Congress does have standing to self-initiate trade cases. I could be wrong about that, but I think that they do. I don't believe this responsibility falls in the mandate of any particular committee.

Obviously, any congressman could request a study, as you've suggested, but I think the issues are broad enough that it would be useful to have an independent commission of the Congress that was charged with investigating dumping and subsidies and other kinds of fair trade violations. So Congress has a unique national interest in the enforcement of fair trade laws.

HEARING CO-CHAIR WESSEL: Commissioner Blumenthal.

COMMISSIONER BLUMENTHAL: Yes. Thank you all very much for interesting testimony.

I want to get to this, I want to unpack a little bit, if possible, the differences between unemployment in the United States and FDI in China. And I don't know how to resolve this. Maybe it's a dispute about statistics, one's statistics. Maybe you could duke it out over statistics.

Besides the loss of the trade bar, which may be productive for the United States, can you explain--no offense to anybody here--if we have three-tenths of one percent of worldwide R&D in China, and the dissection, as you mentioned, Dr. Moran, you have some problems with the dissection of value captured by the iPad, but still so much of it obviously is not captured in places like China--our highest tech goods.

For all of you, and maybe some of you just disagree with this premise, but can you explain which jobs and which sectors are being displaced, and are they being displaced to China? Because we go to a lot of factories in China, and it doesn't seem like Americans would be doing those jobs.

Are they being displaced to Germany where it seems like the American worker is more--that's a better metric of comparison? Are they being not displaced? Or is just a question of productivity gains in the United States? Because I think our manufacturing output was at one of its highest in years in this last year.

So, again, I'd like to get a little bit more educated on the issue of--there's a lot of data flowing around here, but can we get a little bit more granularity on which jobs and which sectors are being displaced to whom? I mean would anyone really be doing these jobs that we see in China that some claim are being displaced? So that's to any of you.

DR. MORAN: I tend to see trade and investment as win/win so I don't immediately start with displaced, and I like competition, which does have some displacement in it. Most of the competition to the manufacturing sector, but increasingly to the service sector, in the United States, comes from other OECD countries.

COMMISSIONER BLUMENTHAL: Right.

DR. MORAN: And so how we fare in comparison to Europe, Japan, and increasingly Korea, or others, is really what the U.S. story is about, and there are some recommendations that I'm--well, I think we all share them--having to do with infrastructure, having to do with education and training, et cetera, that are beyond the scope of this hearing, but that would be where I would put my emphasis.

With regard to displacement of U.S. jobs to China, to the extent that we can measure that, it's a fairly small phenomenon because the main competitors for what China is producing are actually India and Mexico and Brazil and other LDCs.

So you really are not going to be able to take the bilateral U.S.-China and say, well, if their trade balance changed or if something else changed, you would find that jobs would come back to the United States. They may come back to Vietnam or to the Philippines, but I would urge you not to kind of be misled by analogy that displacement is going to be on a bilateral basis.

DR. SCOTT: I would be happy to defend the estimates of jobs displaced by growing trade deficits with China that I published last year. I have looked at the impacts of trade by industry, by state and congressional district. I think about 40 percent of the jobs displaced by the growth in China trade deficits between 2001 and 2008 were in the electronics industries. The three hardest hit congressional districts in the country were in Palo Alto and San Jose, California.

COMMISSIONER BLUMENTHAL: Can I ask a question about that, sir?

DR. SCOTT: Certainly.

COMMISSIONER BLUMENTHAL: So what kinds of jobs? When we go to or see electronics makers in China, these are not the kinds of things you're seeing in the United States, as they're much lower level in terms of skills, and so what kinds of electronics jobs have we lost to China?

DR. SCOTT: Well, my understanding, and I've heard this just informally in comments on the work that I've done, someone referred to San Jose and that area in northern California as "skeleton valley" for all the empty factories that —populate the region.

COMMISSIONER BLUMENTHAL: But have those gone to--

DR. SCOTT: --that used to make computers--

COMMISSIONER BLUMENTHAL: Yes.

DR. SCOTT: --and electronic products that are now being manufactured in China. So we have lost jobs in the past decade in these industries.

COMMISSIONER BLUMENTHAL: Silicon Valley didn't use to manufacture computers. They, again--

DR. SCOTT: Yes, manufacturing computers.

COMMISSIONER BLUMENTHAL: They certainly came up with the designs and so forth, but they didn't--

COMMISSIONER BARTHOLOMEW: They manufactured them.

DR. SCOTT: They did manufacture them, yes.

COMMISSIONER BLUMENTHAL: Not really. Now you're talking about productivity gains, and how much would you break it down to productivity gains? I'm not asking Commissioners for their opinions. I'm asking--and also I'd like Dr. Fung to comment on this as well--the dissection of value capture for Apple iPods so would you agree with the assessment that, I mean is there any way to make a one-to-one comparison between the movement of lower-level component manufacturing in China and the job loss in the United States?

DR. FUNG: I agree with Dr. Moran about the alternative sites of offshoring for all these components and parts and even, for the case of India, some of the service-related activities as well.

However, in terms of not picking China or picking Indonesia or Vietnam, perhaps--I don't have the figures with me--the volume of offshoring activities got magnified because of the interaction of technological improvement as well as the--over the past 30 years--and for India, the past 20 years--the simultaneous rejoining into the global economy by very large, populous, developing economies.

So in that sense, I agree that a lot of these jobs, if it is not in China, it will be in Vietnam.

However, maybe the scope of that kind of offshoring has increased over time, and I see my students, they get more and more--they may be wrong--I don't know--more and more insecure about their job prospects, partly because of the recent financial crisis, but at the same time, there seems to be some sense of unease about this phenomenon that combines technology and emergence of China and India.

DR. SCOTT: I have a paper available that looks at productivity and growth and output and the decline in employment manufacturing. [*See Additional Material for the Record from Robert E. Scott, page 130-131.*] The basic story is that productivity growth has been with us for generations in manufacturing. It grew four percent a year in the '90s, and four percent a year in the past decade. What changed was that output was growing about four percent a year in manufacturing in the 1990s, and demand for manufactured products was growing.

In the past decade, what happened was output only grew about one percent a year. Demand continued to grow. It was just supplied by imports.

And the second point is that China is responsible for about 80 percent of our trade deficit in manufactured products. So China is, for better or worse, the core of the problem.

COMMISSIONER BLUMENTHAL: If we stop trading with China--

HEARING CO-CHAIR WESSEL: Reclaiming the time, I--

COMMISSIONER BLUMENTHAL: I'm sorry. I've got to respond to this or get a clarification. If we stopped trading with China, would we be assembling iPods in the United States?

DR. SCOTT: I think if we had balanced trade with China, we would be producing other products and selling them to them to China, and that's the core of the problem.

HEARING CO-CHAIR WESSEL: Commissioner Bartholomew.

COMMISSIONER BARTHOLOMEW: Thanks very much. Thank you to our witnesses.

Dr. Fung, we don't often get "Banana Slugs" here, so welcome. I'm pleased to see you; and Dr. Moran, it's very nice to note in your biography that your family philanthropy focuses on helping children affected by the HIV-AIDS epidemic. So thank you for the work that you're doing on that. Dr. Scott, it's always wonderful to have you here.

I'm going to take a very brief sliver of my time just to address one thing with Commissioner Blumenthal, which is that the decline in manufacturing is not just these big companies that are putting together things like iPods. If you go anywhere in this country, you can find shut down small and medium-sized businesses and factories that did things like injection plastics or extrusions and/or making tools and dies to make the equipment that make the equipment.

COMMISSIONER BLUMENTHAL: I don't think anyone is arguing that.

COMMISSIONER BARTHOLOMEW: Well, it's--

COMMISSIONER BLUMENTHAL: I think the question is how much, what jobs are actually going to China that would be here?

COMMISSIONER BARTHOLOMEW: Well, I--

COMMISSIONER BLUMENTHAL: It's a completely different question all together. And we have experts here so--

COMMISSIONER BARTHOLOMEW: I didn't want to leave the record implying that though.

But, Dr. Moran, particularly, I'd like to go back to this issue of R&D because I'm trying to understand if it hasn't been working, why is the

Chinese government making so much investment in it through subsidies, these huge R&D parks that they're going--all of the benefits that they're providing? And add in there the caveat that one of the things that we've learned over the past ten years is that the things that happen in China happen much more quickly than we expect that they're going to.

So what is this investment in R&D about?

DR. MORAN: Excellent question. And there is no doubt that China is making a huge investment in higher education, in science parks, in things like that. So that's not subject to dispute. I would have to do further studies of this, or you would have to bring in people who were genuinely expert in this, but my impression of looking at the evidence is many of the graduates of these new universities, et cetera, then go to work for foreign firms.

So you have about 16 million foreign employed workers, a disproportionately high percentage of their exports comes from this. Now, many of them go into domestic firms, indigenous firms, and they're not zero productive; they're just in this--why do I keep pointing to Derek here?

[Laughter.]

DR. MORAN: They're in this messed-up domestic economy, some state-owned, some private- owned firms, and they have some impact. They contribute to the ten percent growth rate. So I don't mean to say nothing is going on there, but my thesis is if you say is China becoming Japan and Germany and Silicon Valley combined, the answer is no, no and no, or so slowly that you really don't see much of it in the data.

COMMISSIONER BARTHOLOMEW: Do you think that is what is behind this indigenous innovation move, this concern that the investments in R&D are not providing the return in terms of Chinese companies being able to take on these activities?

DR. MORAN: I've never seen that be the rationale, but the indigenous innovation is the bad news that your Commission has looked into for years. There really is a kind of design of industrial policy and pressures on GM and pressures on Boeing and pressures on companies to come there, to take on partners, to share their technology, that's very real--I don't quite know how to get at that. But I dislike it just as much as my colleagues do.

COMMISSIONER BARTHOLOMEW: Dr. Fung or Dr. Scott, any comment on the R&D?

DR. FUNG: I'm not an expert on that, but my sense is that China has been disappointed by its perception that it gets stuck in the lower end of the manufacturing activities, and so the big push into science and higher education is perhaps their way of trying to climb up the ladder.

The question is what is the implication for our own labor market, for our own companies? If they're hiring a lot of their own scientists and engineers, would that imply that they're more complementary to our own scientists and engineers or would they displace our own scientists and engineers? I haven't seen studies about that, but obviously it's an area that I'm a little bit concerned about.

COMMISSIONER BARTHOLOMEW: Dr. Scott.

DR. SCOTT: I would emphasize again the role of foreign-owned multinationals in China in doing R&D and its impact. The evidence that I reviewed in my written testimony suggests that foreign-invested enterprises coming from OECD countries are responsible for as much as a third of all GDP growth in China. They're the most productive enterprises in China, and they represent a growing share of the economy in China.

Their share of experts has grown dramatically over time, and they are now bringing with them R&D, and so I think that this is a zero sum game--it's going to come at the expense of workers in the United States, and it's not just those who have low skills, but increasingly those with college degrees and advanced degrees, as well, who are threatened by this migration of investment and R&D to China.

COMMISSIONER BARTHOLOMEW: Thank you.

HEARING CO-CHAIR WESSEL: Vice Chairman Slane.

VICE CHAIRMAN SLANE: Thank you. Thank you all for taking the time to testify. As we all know, the Chinese are offering massive incentives to American high-tech industries to move to China, and let me just give you one example. Evergreen is a manufacturer of solar panels in Devens, Massachusetts, and Evergreen accepted $43 million in aid from the state of Massachusetts and opened up a factory employing 800 workers.

They recently shut the factory down, laid off the 800 workers and moved to China. The CEO said that he could not borrow money at favorable terms in the United States, which would enable his company to grow; the Chinese offered him massive loans at very, very low interest rates.

Our job is to make recommendations to the Congress. Now, my question to you is should the United States government get in the game and start making incentives or countering incentives that the Chinese are offering?

DR. SCOTT: I think that we have to consider that. I think we also have to consider withdrawing from the Government Procurement Agreement of the WTO and using our own public procurement dollars to encourage the development of our own domestic industries. That's part of what China is doing, is it's requiring that green technology is being produced in China. That's one reason the factories are growing so rapidly there, but I do think ultimately we're going to have to compete with China on their terms.

Unfortunately, we're falling behind the rest of the world, and it's not just China; it's Germany; it's France. Other countries around the world provide much more effective support to the development of their industries than we do here in this country.

VICE CHAIRMAN SLANE: Anyone else? Thank you.

HEARING CO-CHAIR WESSEL: Commissioner Mulloy.

COMMISSIONER MULLOY: Thank you, Mr. Chairman, and I want to thank each of the witnesses both for their oral and their very helpful written testimony.

I have a couple questions.. They're related to some things that came up in the earlier panel, but I wanted to get your judgment on it.

We heard earlier that state-owned enterprises get massive subsidies from the Chinese. Even though Huawei may not be officially state owned, it is an enterprise that gets a lot of support from the Chinese government.

We talked about currently these entities can buy things in the United States on the basis--and the only way we could stop them is using the Exon-Florio, which you have to say it's a national security threat, and I mentioned, the Canadians have a different test. You have to show that the purchase is a net benefit to Canada.

Do you folks agree with Derek Scissors and others that that might be a better test for us to have in our own law? I'll start with Dr. Scott and then go across quickly, and then we have another question.

DR. SCOTT: I would agree. I think the Canadian approach is interesting. We should look at alternatives like that. My own research has shown that foreign companies investing in the United States tend to run very large trade deficits. Over the last 20 years, they've displaced over four million workers in the United States.

What many of them do, especially in countries like China, is buy up U.S. companies, close down the factories, use the brand name to market their products here in the United States, and a good example of that might be Lenovo's purchase of IBM's PCs. They're all manufactured abroad. And so I think that this is an issue that we really have to look at quite closely.

COMMISSIONER MULLOY: Dr. Moran? Dr. Fung?

DR. MORAN: I have to say I wish we had more time on this because U.S. MNCs are the largest exporters from the United States, about 60 percent of our exports, and next to them are foreign investors in the United States in terms of size of exports. So I'm not, we have to sort that out.

With regard to a net benefits test, I am very much opposed to that, not because it isn't a good idea, but because it is an opportunity for mischief that I think would be very ill-advised.

COMMISSIONER MULLOY: Okay. Dr. Fung.

DR. FUNG: I guess economists generally are in favor of the views of net benefits to assess policies even though I understand that politically sometimes they get a little bit messed up.

COMMISSIONER MULLOY: Thank you.

The second question, you can belong to the WTO without belonging to the Government Procurement Agreement of the WTO. For example, China belongs to the WTO but is not part of the Government Procurement Agreement.

We signed on to the GPA voluntarily. Some of the states also signed on at the urging of the national government. Some of the states have now withdrawn their own--because it's a voluntary agreement--because they said this isn't a good deal for us. Does anyone know of any studies that show that we get a benefit from belonging to the GPA?

Secondly, is there a problem as the Congressman, two congressmen talked about, a Chinese entities building the helicopters for the President, and that these entities are subsidized by the Chinese government and, therefore, get an unfair competitive advantage?

Would the United States be better off withdrawing from the GPA unless we can show some way that we're getting massive benefits from belonging to it?

And I'll start with Dr. Scott and then go across.

DR. SCOTT: I have already suggested that withdrawing from the GPA would be useful. I think we are almost alone again in the world in allowing our government purchases to be used to purchase products from all over the world. Even in countries who signed on to the Agreement, many of our European partners, for example, although they've signed the Agreement, somehow it ends up much of their domestic government purchasing is done domestically. So they somehow use those resources to benefit domestic industries.

COMMISSIONER MULLOY: Dr. Moran.

DR. MORAN: I'm sorry. I'm not an expert on the evidence about government procurement. I have to say the idea of the Chinese building the President's helicopter strikes me as a ridiculous idea, just on security grounds alone, not on expense or subsidy or whatever.

COMMISSIONER MULLOY: Thank you.

Dr. Fung?

DR. FUNG: I guess since the perception is about Chinese government using government procurement to favor domestic firms, I wonder if one can think about using some parts of that policy in the U.S., as well, as a bargaining chip? I don't know about it. So--thank you.

COMMISSIONER MULLOY: Thank you.

On the other part of my question, let me come back. Hopefully, we'll have another chance. Thank you both, all of you.

HEARING CO-CHAIR WESSEL: Commissioner Brookes.

COMMISSIONER BROOKES: Thank you and thank you all for being here.

It's been alluded to a few times in brief moments throughout the testimony and the questioning, but I'd really like to ask all of you, and perhaps Dr. Moran had already spoken to this a little bit more than the others, but what effect do you think that Beijing's indigenous innovation policy will have on China's economic competitiveness. We've had some promises during President Hu Jintao's recent visit, but where do you think the Chinese are going with that policy?

Thank you.

DR. MORAN: I'm opposed to it. I would welcome--if they actually say they're not going to do it, and they head in that direction, I think that would be spectacular. But there are so many interests in trying to force technology transfer that I'll believe it when I see it, not just rely on statements.

COMMISSIONER BROOKES: Dr. Scott? Dr. Fung?

DR. SCOTT: I would agree. I think China has shown that is has very creatively used a wide range of government policies to encourage multinationals to transfer technology to joint ventures and domestic partners. And I think they will continue to do that, especially in the new green technology industries they've targeted for development. So, I agree with Dr. Moran--actions speak much louder than words, especially when dealing with China. We see many oral commitments in the past that haven't amounted to much, especially in the technology area, from the Chinese.

DR. FUNG: I think I agree with the other presenters that indigenous innovation policy is going to be bad for China's prospects for long-term growth. Unfortunately, there may be situations that bad policies like this one in China may also be bad for some of our companies as well.

COMMISSIONER BROOKES: Dr. Fung, why do you think it's going to affect China's prospects as opposed to those of the foreign--

DR. FUNG: My interpretation of the high growth of China was because of their successful economic reform choice, marketization, and opening up to foreign firms, more or less preserve some degree of competition among various parties and companies. So now they started to favor a particular group of companies, my understanding is part of these sectors and companies are politically-connected, and not solely based on merits, so in the long-run, that seems to me not very conducive to economic growth.

COMMISSIONER BROOKES: So you're saying that the indigenous innovation policy may stifle Chinese efforts at innovation and competitiveness?

DR. FUNG: That would be my conjecture for the long-run for China.

COMMISSIONER BROOKES: Dr. Moran or Dr. Scott, do you have any views on that?

DR. MORAN: No.

COMMISSIONER BROOKES: Okay.

DR. SCOTT: I'm skeptical. I think that China has been very effective at extracting technology from other companies and using it, my interpretation is the indigenous innovation policies will be used to simply encourage more of that transfer of technology. I don't think they're going to give up with working with foreign companies. I think they want to make sure that more of the innovation happens in China.

COMMISSIONER BROOKES: The argument that I understand that's being presented, and I think Dr. Fung and I are talking about, is that the transfer of technology will actually inhibit or stifle Chinese innovation because they're just having the technology transferred. They're not putting the time and effort into developing new technologies or innovation, and Dr. Fung, if I understood him correctly, believes that ultimately it will stifle Chinese innovation as opposed to advance it.

Is that your view as well, Dr. Scott?

DR. SCOTT: China is in the process of catching up with Western technology. Their level of productivity is still far behind the United States. They've got a GDP of about $4 trillion. U.S. GDP is about $14 trillion. They have about four times as many people as we do. So catching up can take them a long, long way, and I think China is a long way from the technical frontier. It may be a long time before not being able to produce all the cutting-edge technologies is going to be costly for them.

COMMISSIONER BROOKES: Thank you.

HEARING CO-CHAIR WESSEL: Chairman Reinsch.

CHAIRMAN REINSCH: Thank you.

First, I want to thank Commissioner Blumenthal for bringing up the question about the disposition of jobs. I'm reasonably confident he and I don't agree on what to do about it, but I think it's an important question. We've been--

COMMISSIONER BLUMENTHAL: Let me be the judge of that.

[Laughter.]

CHAIRMAN REINSCH: I'm not going to tell you what I think, but we've been losing jobs for a long time.

COMMISSIONER BLUMENTHAL: I can't disagree with that.

CHAIRMAN REINSCH: The question of not so much where they're going, but what they are, whether they would come back, depending upon what policies we would pursue, and whether it's more important to try to bring them back, or more important to create new ones, which may not be mutually exclusive policies, are really important questions. So I appreciate the panel's comment on that.

I've got a different line I want to pursue. Ted, you began by talking about spillovers and the absence of spillovers in your comments, and I'd like to pursue that for just a minute. You concluded that there wasn't much, and we've just been talking about indigenous innovation, and Dr. Scott essentially said the Chinese have been fairly effective at forcing what is, in effect, a spillover.

First, I assume whether there are any spillovers or not, there's significant pressure on companies to do that. So question one is do you agree with Dr. Scott or do you want to comment on the indigenous innovation issue in light of what you said earlier?

And second, how do companies go about resisting the kinds of pressures that are put on them?

DR. MORAN: Well, there clearly are two opposing things going on at the same time. If you look at high-speed rail, for example, this is probably the poster child of effectively using pressures and joint ventures to create reverse engineer, learn, go up the learning curve, and then take over an industry. And it has happened.

If you look at aerospace, you see the same pressures being put on Boeing or on Airbus. I am skeptical that they're going to replace Boeing or Airbus any time in the near future even though they're trying to move up, as Dr. Scott said, the learning curve. So I think they're still going to be behind the frontier for a long time.

They're not going to do in aerospace what they did in--

CHAIRMAN REINSCH: Well, let me interrupt you there for a minute. Is there a difference between replacing Boeing or Airbus or, alternatively, developing a commercially viable wide-body aircraft that competes in the marketplace?

DR. MORAN: I'm sure they will do that eventually. Well, that competes in the marketplace is a question--

CHAIRMAN REINSCH: Besides their marketplace.

DR. MORAN: Yes. They're going to have shortly some kind of aviation equipment, and the planes will get bigger and bigger. Will they become competitive? It's a fairly competitive industry so it's going to be hard. Am I worried that they're going to displace Boeing and Airbus? No.

The other disconnect is to look across the broad array of high-performance electronics, industrial equipment, medical equipment, and then you look at the statistics, both survey data and econometric data, and you find that either horizontal spillovers or vertical spillovers aren't taking place.

And the domestic value-added isn't increasing, and the Chinese don't seem to be learning by doing. And the Chinese exporters, are they catching up with FDI exporters? The answer is no, they are falling further behind. So for reasons having to do with distortion and lack of human resources, and despite what you said about all the universities and the research centers, they're not using FDI to transform their indigenous economy very rapidly.

CHAIRMAN REINSCH: Thank you.

Dr. Scott, in your original statement, you talked about the need to search for new ways to address unfair trade practice, dumping subsidies, things like that, or, alternatively, I guess leave the WTO dispute settlement process.

A lot of people have thought about that for a long time. Do you have any suggestions as to what those new ideas might be?

DR. SCOTT: In terms of?

CHAIRMAN REINSCH: U.S. law.

DR. SCOTT: Well, in my written statement I've outlined a number of ways in which I think we could change U.S. law. Just take a couple of specific examples.

On dumping, one of the problems we have with dumping is now

domestic industries have to prove that they've been injured in order to qualify for antidumping remedies. Usually, the industry has to show that it's actually losing money. So you find that there's a surge in dumping cases during recessions, and that's about the only time a domestic industry can get the ITC to give to issue an affirmative antidumping decision.

And yet, as an economist, I know that when imports surge, and they reduce prices and profit and employment, that causes economic injury. Now companies may still be making money, they may earn a minimal profit in the situation, but they're clearly suffering injury.

So one thing you could do is change the legal definition of "injury." That's something I've worked on; I've consulted on; I've had some experience with that.

CHAIRMAN REINSCH: I'd love to continue this, but my time is up. Thank you.

HEARING CO-CHAIR WESSEL: Commissioner Shea.

COMMISSIONER SHEA: Thank all of you for being here and for your interesting testimony.

Thank you, Dr. Moran, for bringing up this issue of advanced technology exports. As I understand your testimony, you said approximately 96 percent of the exports from China to the United States in the Advanced Technology Product category are manufactured by foreign-invested enterprises in China. Is that right?

DR. MORAN: Yes.

COMMISSIONER SHEA: And then you say that the Chinese ATP imports from the United States are the high-end sophisticated products, and that the Chinese--what China exports from these foreign-invested enterprises based in China to the United States are essentially low end.

As I understand it, the U.S. ran a trade surplus with China in Advanced Technology Products in 2003. I think it was a modest two or $3 billion trade surplus. But most recently, it is running a significant deficit. I don't know what their exact number--60, $70 billion trade deficit.

What does that mean? Are the foreign-invested enterprises just based in China sending us a lot more of those high school lab microscopes, and we're sending them, China, a lot fewer high-end physics microscopes? How do you unpack that for us?

DR. MORAN: Well, I hate to say we'd actually have to look at the data. I don't know. I think the way you've characterized it must be what's going on because you have very well presented kind of what the data looked like.

So I can't, go any further. That seems to me what's happening. That is to say the foreign-invested companies are doing more and more of this, but they're not doing it at the very highest end in China.

COMMISSIONER SHEA: Dr. Scott, do you want to weigh in on this?

DR. SCOTT: The United States did have a surplus in Advanced Technology Products until about 2002. It now has an overall deficit of about

$50 billion. That's entirely due to the ATP trade deficit with China. We have a trade surplus in Advanced Technology Products with the rest of the world. So China really stands out as being unique in that regard.

It's not just microscopes. It's also, most importantly, in computer products and telecommunications equipment. Those are the areas where China really dominates production. I'm not convinced that these are all low-technology products, by any means. I think China is moving up the food chain, and it's a real threat.

I think the larger question is if we were just trading low-tech products with China and exporting high-tech products to China, that's great in theory; both sides win. The reality is we import lots of everything from China, and primarily what we export to China are raw materials like plastic, and our third largest export to China is scrap, steel and paper scrap.

So those are not high-tech commodities, particularly scrap. That doesn't generate a lot of jobs.

COMMISSIONER SHEA: Dr. Moran, when you talk about the low end of the ATP value-added chain in your testimony, what products are you talking about there just so that I have an understanding?

DR. MORAN: The measurements are in terms of skill intensity so I'd have to actually go back and look at the product categories. I'm sorry that I can't--

COMMISSIONER SHEA: Does it raise a red flag for you that we have gone from a surplus situation with China on Advanced Technology Products now to a significant deficit? Does that raise any concerns with you?

DR. MORAN: That sounds like a trick question.   COMMISSIONER SHEA: No, I'm not trying to trick you, I promise.

DR. MORAN: Because I see the benefits from the foreign investment flowing back to the United States. So--

COMMISSIONER SHEA: I'm just trying to understand.

DR. MORAN: Yes. I'm not finding that real worrisome. Now, if I can introduce something that none of us have talked about, and that is trade in services.

I share the concern about the manufacturing base so this is not an either/or. I like the manufacturing base, but the big growth there--and I like Commissioner Reinsch's create new jobs versus try and bring back old jobs way of thinking about this. The United States is the powerhouse of high-tech services, and that goes from engineering services to construction services to business services to management services to academic professorial services--thank you very much.

And it's growing very rapidly. We are doing some outsourcing, and some of your students, like my students, are afraid that they might. But the huge potential with China as well as elsewhere is our potential exports of services.

COMMISSIONER SHEA: Thank you very much.

HEARING CO-CHAIR WESSEL: Commissioner Cleveland.

COMMISSIONER CLEVELAND: Thank you, all.

We've talked about the FDI's impact on jobs and tech transfer and the overall GDP in China, but what we haven't talked about is why U.S. companies are investing as heavily as they are. I think we all agree that China's aggressive policies when it comes to subsidies and tax benefits and certainly labor costs is an element that attracts U.S. companies.

But I'm wondering if the idea of a 1.3 billion person consumer market is a myth? Let me leave it at that for a moment.

And then a related question is has the priority of American companies shifted somewhat, and it's less about the immediacy of the opportunity in Chinese markets, and they are, in fact, using China as a platform for exports to Southeast Asia?

Any of you?

DR. MORAN: Could you give another sentence about the myth? I was following you up to the--

COMMISSIONER CLEVELAND: Well, I think that American companies are not stupid, and they're in this for a reason. They're investing in China not just because there are all kinds of tax and other subsidies offered. I think there continues to be a perception that there's a real market here, and the entire discussion today has focused on why they are attracted to invest in China and not so much about the market opportunities.

And I'm wondering if you think that those market opportunities are real or they're just caught up in the notion that the subsidies are so attractive that they can't afford not to invest? Why are they there?

DR. MORAN: I'll go first. The growth of the consumer market in China is certainly not a myth, and the rise of the middle class is going to be the story of the next 20 years in China. And we've already heard about the relative profitability of firms; it has to be risk-adjusted, as you rightly point out. So, yes, I think they're investing to be in China.

Your second question, is it a platform for Southeast Asia. There's a lot of evidence that says, yes, there really is development of complex supply chains within Southeast Asia, which China is just a component. So both of those are happening.

Now, we've heard a lot of testimony about the subsidies, and low cost interest, and--

COMMISSIONER CLEVELAND: Labor.

DR. MORAN: --about Evergreen moving from Massachusetts, and all that rings true and is bad. We don't like that, but I doubt that most of the firms are making their decisions on the basis solely of where they can get subsidies.

DR. SCOTT: To go to your myth question, I think we've been hearing this claim about the great growing consumer market in Country X for almost 20 years now. We heard that first about Mexico in NAFTA. Well, that hasn't proved to be of any great benefit to the United States. We have a large and growing trade deficit with Mexico.

The same is true with China. Most of what we export to China are inputs into goods that are going to be reexported back to the United States and other developed country markets. Multinationals are investing in China to export primarily to rich country markets. That's where the profits are, and that's what this is about.

Retained earnings, globally, earned by U.S. multinationals, have increased 186 percent between 1999 and 2010, according to U.S. data. Those are global data. But investing abroad is extraordinarily profitable, and when it comes to investing in China, it's all about producing for export and outsourcing jobs from the U.S. to that location, in my view.

COMMISSIONER CLEVELAND: Dr. Fung, do you have anything to add?

DR. FUNG: I agree with the other presenters, but in addition to that, sometimes the consumers need not be individuals, it can be companies, including SOEs. I met a businessman in Oregon, and he was selling grass seeds, which I didn't know there was a market for grass seeds.

But he said now China is the biggest market. A lot of the cities were trying--including second-tier cities--were trying to combat pollution, as well as sometimes with sports events, they need to beautify their cities.

So the local governments and the provincial governments were spending a lot of money to purchase grass seeds to grow grass. So it's not just 1.3 billion, but also maybe some government entities could be the buyers as well.

COMMISSIONER CLEVELAND: Thank you.

HEARING CO-CHAIR WESSEL: For a brief question, Commissioner Mulloy.

COMMISSIONER MULLOY: Thank you, Mr. Chairman. Thank you for the witnesses.

Dr. Fung, on page three of your prepared testimony, you make this point: U.S. direct investment increases Chinese output, and other FDI also increases Chinese output, but you say U.S. direct investment seemed to be more potent than investment from Hong Kong, Japan, Taiwan or the Republic of Korea.

Can you quickly give us why you think that is the case? And then I have a question for the other two witnesses to comment on.

COMMISSIONER CLEVELAND: No, you only get one.

DR. FUNG: This is from statistical study, but our interpretation was that a lot of the management practices, the technology, as well as other ways to organize the business, serve as important lessons for the rest of the Chinese economy and so increase the aggregate output in China.

COMMISSIONER MULLOY: More effective from U.S. companies than these other companies?

DR. FUNG: According to the statistical study.

HEARING CO-CHAIR WESSEL: Thank you to the witnesses. We will be breaking until one o'clock, at which point we will have our third panel. Thank you.

[Whereupon, at 12:19 p.m., the hearing recessed, to reconvene at 1:02 p.m., this same day.]

A F T E R N O O N   S E S S I O N

PANEL IV: CHINESE INVESTMENTS IN THE UNITED STATES

HEARING CO-CHAIR WESSEL: We'll get started, and some of the other Commissioners are still detained and will trickle in over the next couple of minutes.

Our third and final panel for the day is on "Chinese Investments in the United States." We have two witnesses:

Mr. Daniel Rosen is a Principal and China Practice Leader at the Rhodium Group, a New York-based research firm. He is also Visiting Fellow at the Peterson Institute for International Economics and adjunct professor at Columbia University's School of International and Public Affairs.

Mr. Rosen was a member of the National Economic Council staff from 2000 to 2001, where he served as a senior advisor for international economic policy.

His work has focused on the economic development of East Asia, particularly greater China, and U.S. economic relations with the region. Other areas of research include energy, agriculture and commodities, trade and environment linkages, and economic transitions and competitiveness.

Mr. Rosen appeared before the Commission in 2007 at the hearing on "Government Control of the Chinese Economy."

Dr. Sauvant is the Founder and Executive Director of the Vale Columbia Center on Sustainable International Investment.

He also serves as a Senior Research Scholar and Lecturer in Law at Columbia Law School; the Co-Director of the Millennium Cities Initiative; Senior Advisor on the Investment Advisory Committee of the China International Investment Council, formerly the China Federation of Investment Promotion Agencies; and is a member of the International Advisory Council of CUNY's International Center for Corporate Accountability.

Until July 2005, he was the Director of the United Nations Conference on Trade and Development's Division on Investment, Technology and Enterprise Development.

Our normal rule is roughly seven minutes oral testimony.   Your prepared testimony will be made a part of the record.

Dr. Rosen, if you can begin.

STATEMENT OF MR. DANIEL H. ROSEN
PRINCIPAL, RHODIUM GROUP, LLC, AND
VISITING FELLOW, PETERSON INSTITUTE OF INTERNATIONAL ECONOMICS,
NEW YORK, NEW YORK

MR. ROSEN: Commissioner Wessel, thank you very much and to the other members for the invitation to join you for this timely panel.

My colleagues and I at Rhodium Group have been working on this issue, including the state-owned enterprise aspects of this issue, for some time. In fact, most immediately, the past five years, we've been watching China's global outbound direct investment numbers go up. Presently, we're looking very much at how they're going up to the United States, in particular.

We have a book coming out May 4 here in Washington sponsored by the Asia Society on that topic, and a larger study on China's global outbound direct investment footprint out from the Peterson Institute at the end of the year.

Based on that research, I think I can help answer some of the questions which your staff and you put together for us to think about here today. In the opening portion here, I'll offer a few of the numbers in the research we have coming out soon and touch on a couple of the key conclusions that we're coming to in our work.

First, on the numbers, it's clear from the questions that you posed, first of all, that our interest here today is direct investment, not portfolio investment, although we can pull that into the conversation as well.

Today, the value of Chinese direct investment in the United States is very, very modest. One-tenth of one percent of all the foreign direct investment in the United States is coming from China, according to the official BEA numbers, and also according to official estimates, Chinese total holdings of U.S. Treasury bills and other portfolio securities are about 700 times greater than that value of Chinese foreign direct investment in the U.S.

But with the benefit of an alternative methodology for trying to add up the value of direct investment from China that my colleague Thilo Hanemann and I have worked out and are employing in our work, we can see that an upward inflection in the annual flows to the United States has already very much started. It's very much visible.

I'm happy to go into the methodology later if you're interested, but what's most important to recognize at the outset is that our alternative number is different because, unlike BEA data that looks at the net inflow of FDI, we're looking at the new capital formation on the asset side by ultimately Chinese companies. So we're asking "what's the value of assets held by Chinese firms in America"?

We're not asking what's the net FDI position after Chinese companies establish here and then make a loan back to their headquarters in China so it doesn't show up as an increase in the net U.S. FDI position.

So that's how our approach is different. It's supplemental to what the BEA gives us to work with and provides a different look at what's happening. By our account, therefore, in both 2009 and 2010, China's assets in the U.S. increase by 130 percent a year, year over year.

The full-year 2010 flow was in the vicinity of $5.5 billion, bringing the accumulated Chinese FDI position in the U.S. to roughly $11.6 billion since 2003.

A major virtue of our granular bottom-up tally of the FDI numbers from China is that we can observe many characteristics and patterns that are hard to see in the traditional balance of payments data, and let me mention what three of those patterns are that we see.

First, we find that about 75 percent of the 244 individual Chinese direct investments that we record since 2003 were done by private or publicly-held Chinese companies, not government-controlled entities.

In terms of value, the government-firm share in the U.S. is higher because the SOEs are in the more capital-intensive industries, as I'm sure Dr. Scissors pointed out. But in terms of number, it's mostly private companies that are coming to America.

Secondly, the sectoral distribution of the investment is very broad. There's greater than $100 million in Chinese direct investment in no fewer than 16 different U.S. industries, ten of them manufacturing; six, services. The picture of China only going after and cherry-picking a small handful of sensitive industries is not, in fact, accurate when we look at the data.

Third, in terms of the investment structure approach being used, there's also diversity. There's no indication of a coordinated template for approaching the U.S. investment market by Chinese firms. Chinese investments are more or less evenly split between greenfield investment overtures and merger and acquisition transactions, which is a somewhat surprising reality given the common assumption that making greenfield investments is too challenging for most Chinese firms.

There are many other data fields of interest in the work we have coming out soon, and I'd be happy to preview as much as I can of that for you.

Turning to the policy and the politics, something else both in your question set and in the work we're putting out soon, many of the Commission's questions concern the effectiveness and coverage of U.S. regimes and regulations governing foreign direct investment from China.

As far as my initial summary, I would say that Chinese direct investment is today well screened for national security considerations under existing U.S. law and policy processes.

I do not perceive flaws in U.S. policy which would permit specific threats to slip through which would be prevented by a better regulatory regime than what we have today.

On the other hand, I am actually greatly concerned that incendiary politicization of specific investments and overzealous insinuation of mal-intent can and do interfere with the efficient functioning of the national security screening process that we've built over decades and decades of dealing with our partners in the international economy.

When we talk about the adequacy of U.S. policy, we usually talk just about the screening process that I just commented on. However, we're starting to think that the time has come to add to that discussion an appraisal of the positive efforts we're making. That is whether we're doing everything we should be doing to actively promote the right kind of job creating/tax-base enhancing Chinese investment in the United States.

Surely, a review of what we're doing on that front is currently indicated. The traditional laissez-faire approach we've taken at the national level, which presumed the United States was the most attractive destination in the world, we didn't have do anything, leave it to the states, it's probably time we reconsider that.

I'm out of time so if I can have just 30 more seconds, I will mention two of our most important conclusions in the longer study. The first is that we've lost control of the narrative that we should have control of. Two years in a row of more than 100 percent year-on-year growth in Chinese investment, large Chinese investments across 16 U.S. industries, the story ought to be that the United States is open to Chinese investment; we don't mess around with this the way some other countries do.

Instead, the narrative in China and here is why is the United States refusing to open up to Chinese investors, and what are we going to do to guarantee our friends in Beijing that we're going to play fair? It's just absurd, I think, that we've allowed the narrative to be lost in the way we have.

And second, and finally, some here in Washington and elsewhere will be concerned that a diagnosis that the direct investment flows from China are going up dramatically means they must be selling down their U.S. debt Treasurys position, and it is an alarm bell on that front.

In fact, for the time being, both China's holding of U.S. government debt and its direct investment position are going up strongly. So that is an issue we may have to confront and be concerned with for the future. It's not the issue we need to be concerned with right now.

I would say that as long as the United States is the most attractive polity in the world, people will buy our government debt. As long as our economy is the most competitive and dynamic and innovative in the world, people will want to do direct investment here. We can have both. It's not an either/or that we have to worry about tradeoffs on.

   That's it for my initial comments. Thanks for the extra minute.

   [The written statement follows:]

PREPARED STATEMENT OF MR. DANIEL H. ROSEN
PRINCIPAL, RHODIUM GROUP, LLC, AND
VISITING FELLOW, PETERSON INSTITUTE OF INTERNATIONAL ECONOMICS, NEW YORK, NEW YORK

Vice Chairman Slane, Commissioner Wessel, members of the Commission: thank you for this opportunity to participate in a very timely hearing.

My colleagues at the Rhodium Group and I have been following and analyzing China's outward investment for more than 5 years. In June 2009, we published a Peterson Institute policy brief on the drivers and policy implications of these new investment flows, which I have submitted to the record. This year we will release 2 more studies on the topic, starting in early May with an analysis of Chinese direct investment in the United States co-sponsored by the Asia Society and the Woodrow Wilson Center for Scholars. Based on this research I can help answer a number of the questions you have set out for this hearing. In this opening statement I will present up to date numbers on Chinese investment and address questions about our policy processes, and then summarize several important conclusions from our current work.

1. The Numbers

It is clear from the questions posed by the Commission that your interest today is in direct investment, as opposed to portfolio investment. Today the value of Chinese direct investment in the US is very modest, representing just 0.1 percent of all foreign direct investment (FDI) in the US. According to official estimates, total Chinese holdings of US treasury bills and other portfolio securities are 700 times greater than China's FDI assets in the US, so the latter is indeed still marginal.

But with the benefit of real-time methodologies such as we have chosen to employ in our current work we can see that an upward inflection in the annual flows has already started. I am happy to go into that methodology later, but it is important to point out at the start that we elect to measure *Chinese controlled assets* in the US, not just net-FDI inflows.

In both 2009 and 2010 China's FDI in the US increased 130% year-on-year. The full year 2010 flow was in the vicinity of $5.3 billion, bringing the accumulated Chinese direct investment in the US to roughly $11.6 billion since 2003. A major virtue of our granular, bottom-up tally of Chinese FDI deals in the US is that we can observe many characteristics and patterns that are hard to see in traditional balance of payments (BOP) data. Let me preview 3 for you:

First, we have found that 75% of the 244 Chinese investments in the US that we recorded between 2003 and 2010 were done by private or publicly held firms, as opposed to government-controlled companies. In terms of value, the government-owned share is higher, but in both cases the share of government-controlled firms is lower than that for Chinese investment globally.

Second, the sectoral distribution of this investment is very broad. There is greater than $100 million in Chinese direct investment in no fewer than 16 different US industries; 10 of these are manufacturing-related and 6 are service. These range from higher-technology industries to less sophisticated.

Third, in terms of the investment structures used, there is also great diversity: there is no indication of a coordinated template for approaching the US investment market. Chinese investments are more or less evenly split between greenfield overtures and mergers and acquisitions (M&A), a somewhat surprising reality given the common assumption that making greenfield investments is too challenging for most Chinese firms.

There are many other data fields in our work which we hope to have completed and available for presentation within 6 weeks. However I wish to add one critical qualitative characterization to these quantitative metrics now: namely, that commercial forces are the most significant driver of the upward inflection in US direct investment by Chinese firms we are observing today.

2. The Policy and Politics

A number of the Commission's questions concern the effectiveness and coverage of US regimes and regulations governing foreign direct investment from China. We explore this topic at length in our forthcoming work and I would be pleased to respond to your specific questions today.

As an initial summary, I would say that Chinese direct investment is well screened for national security considerations under existing US law and policy processes. I do not perceive flaws in US policy which would permit specific threats to slip through, which would be prevented by a "better" regulatory regime. On the other hand, I am greatly concerned that incendiary politicization of specific investments and over-zealous insinuation of mal-intent can and do interfere with efficient functioning of the national security screening process.

When we talk about the adequacy of US policy, we are usually talking about the screening process that I just commented on. However the time has come to add to the discussion an appraisal of the positive side of our policy efforts, that is, whether we are doing everything we should be doing to actively *promote* direct investment, including Chinese, in the United States. We think that a review of our efforts to attract Chinese investment is needed. The current laissez-faire approach stems from an era when the US dominated global FDI flows, and assumes the US is unrivaled in its attractiveness, and that our foreign investors come from similar countries and don't need on the ground assistance. That situation has changed. More proactive measures not just at the state and local level, where earnest efforts are afoot, but at the national level to reduce barriers and increase the attraction of the US economy now need to be considered.

3. Most Important Conclusions

I will finish my initial remarks by summarizing two conclusions from our forthcoming study. The unintended consequences of interference in the screening process is the first. With 2010 Chinese investment in the US up 130% year on year, the Chinese public should be singing the praises of the United States as a role model for international investment openness. Instead, as a result of hostile allegations from various interested parties inside and outside the US government concerning deals which in some cases involve no national security concerns whatsoever, the perception in China today is that the US is using FDI screening to pursue mercantilist objectives. That is highly regrettable, for many reasons, including the irony of such appearances coming from China, and the fact that protectionists in China are handed a perfect excuse to initiate similar screening of US investments in China which have never formally been imposed before. In dollar terms, precise numbers are hard to offer, but I think it is safe to say that poisoning the US atmosphere for Chinese investors would likely divert tens of billions of dollars of capital from American states and towns to beneficiaries in Canada, Europe, Japan and other competing economies between now and 2020.

Second, and finally, I would like to point out that direct investment is not a substitute for portfolio investment. The growth of direct investment in the US by Chinese firms does not imply a reduction in Chinese Treasury bill holdings. One does not simply switch out of bonds and into bricks and mortar assets which must be run in compliance with foreign laws, cultures and business conditions. Further, as our methodology makes explicit, the value of Chinese assets in the US includes local financing, not just cash brought in from Beijing. If US government debt remains the most reliable store of value in the world, then China – both sovereign and private – will continue to hold it; if the US market remains the most innovative, largest and attractive in the world, then Chinese firms – both state-related and private – will seek to make direct investments here. This is not an either/or phenomenon.

There are a great number of other points of interest on this topic which I believe are worth your attention, and I do hope we will have an opportunity to explore many of those in question and answer.

Thank you.

> HEARING CO-CHAIR WESSEL: Thank you.
> Doctor.

STATEMENT OF DR. KARL P. SAUVANT
EXECUTIVE DIRECTOR, VALE COLUMBIA CENTER ON SUSTAINABLE
INTERNATIONAL INVESTMENT, COLUMBIA UNIVERSITY
NEW YORK, NEW YORK

DR. SAUVANT: Mr. Chairman, distinguished Commissioners, ladies and gentlemen, it is an honor for me to testify before the U.S.-China Economic and Security Review Commission.

Like Dan, permit me, please, to focus my remarks on foreign direct investment. World foreign direct investment flows have grown from an average of about $50 billion during the first half of the 1980s to $2 trillion in 2007, before they declined to $1 trillion in 2009-2010 as a result of the crisis.

Traditionally, the United States has been the leading host and home country--in other words, the largest importer and exporter of foreign direct investment. And partly because of that, traditionally the U.S. has been a leader in establishing a strong and open international investment law regime that protects foreign direct investment and even encourages it, with the principle of nondiscrimination playing a particularly important role. The reason is that foreign direct investment plays an important role in strengthening the competitiveness of firms and in contributing to development.

This approach has gained widespread approval by virtually all countries in the world, and has indeed led to a strong international investment law and policy regime. And the U.S., as I have mentioned, has benefited particularly from it because it has been, for the reason that Dan indicated, the most attractive host and home country. It is, therefore, surprising to see that there is so widespread skepticism regarding Chinese FDI in the United States. This is all the more surprising since this investment is very small indeed, as we have heard. Inflows were around $1 billion in 2009, according to official U.S. Department of Commerce figures; U.S. flows to China that year were about $4 billion. With foreign direct

104

investment inflows into the U.S. amounting $129 billion in 2009, China's share was less, considerably less, than one percent.

However, and this is atypical if compared to other countries, some 80 to 90 percent of the value of foreign direct investment, not necessarily the number of foreign affiliates, from China is undertaken by state-owned enterprises. At the same time, though, there is little, if any, systematic evidence that state-owned enterprises, be they headquartered in China, Singapore, France, Germany, or any other country, behave differently from private multinationals when they undertake foreign direct investment projects abroad.

It is, of course, true that Chinese firms face considerable challenges when establishing and operating foreign affiliates in the United States that have little or nothing to do with any skepticism regarding foreign direct investment from China. Rather, they are the result of the inexperience of Chinese firms. After all, they became active in the world foreign direct investment market in a significant manner only since the year 2000 when China launched its going global policy.

Chinese multinationals, like all multinationals, face the "liability of foreignness" challenge, that is, the challenge of operating as foreigners in a foreign market. For Chinese firms, this challenge is particularly high given the regulatory and institutional differences and gap between China and the U.S. Chinese firms simply don't have the experience of how to become quickly accepted insiders in a host country that contributes to the economic and social development in the communities in which they are established.

This disadvantage can be accentuated by the "liability of the home country", that is, Chinese firms establishing themselves in the U.S. may be regarded differently than, say, UK firms that do the same.

Mr. Chairman, let me conclude by offering four recommendations. First, the U.S. should strive to maintain its role as a leader in establishing a strong and open international investment law and policy regime to make sure that the rule of law governs foreign direct investment between countries. In particular, the principle of nondiscrimination, the heart of the international investment law regime, should be respected and promoted. The Chinese-U.S. BIT that is under negotiation may offer an excellent opportunity to further strengthen this principle of nondiscrimination.

Two, at the same time, I suggest that the international law and policy regime (and the national FDI regimes require some rebalancing to allow governments to pursue legitimate public policy objectives regarding their own essential security interests or, broader, their national interests. But an effort needs to be made to define or circumscribe as clearly as possible what the concepts of "essential security interests" and "national interests" mean to avoid that they are being used--or abused--for protectionist purposes.

Three, outward investment from China is growing, as we have heard. In fact, China was in the year 2009 the world's fifth largest outward investor. And the U.S. should seek to attract as much of this investment as possible, and in this I echo entirely what Dan has said. (It would, of course, face stiff competition from other countries that seek to attract the same investment, but it certainly is worth a try.) The U.S. should welcome Chinese foreign direct investment, but at the same time make sure that it, like foreign direct investment from any other country, obeys scrupulously U.S. laws and regulations. Such an approach by the United States and other countries would also contribute toward integrating China into the world economy and making it a responsible stakeholder in it.

Fourth and finally, given that China's multinational enterprises are young and relatively inexperienced, we should find ways of helping them to become good corporate citizens in the U.S., not only to avoid unnecessary frictions, but also to increase the contribution that Chinese foreign direct investment can make to the U.S. economy and society.

By way of conclusion, Mr. Chairman, let me remind us all that we had a similar situation some 25 years ago when Japanese firms emerged as major outward investors. Like today, vis-a-vis Chinese firms, there was a strong reaction against the new kids on the block, so to speak, in light of a range of concerns. In fact, CFIUS was created at that time and in reaction to incoming Japanese investment. We managed to integrate and accept Japanese foreign direct investment and benefit from it, and in fact, we are actively seeking it. I trust that over time we will have the same experience with Chinese foreign direct investment in the United States.

Thank you very much for your attention.

[The written statement follows:]

PREPARED STATEMENT OF DR. KARL P. SAUVANT
EXECUTIVE DIRECTOR, VALE COLUMBIA CENTER ON SUSTAINABLE INTERNATIONAL INVESTMENT, COLUMBIA UNIVERSITY
NEW YORK, NEW YORK

Mr. Chairman, ladies and gentlemen.

My name is Karl P. Sauvant, and I am the Executive Director of the Vale Columbia Center on Sustainable International Investment, a joint center of Columbia Law School and the Earth Institute at Columbia University in the City of New York. It is an honor for me to testify before the US- China Economic and Security Review Commission.

Permit me, please, to focus my remarks on foreign direct investment (FDI), i.e. investment that gives a company headquartered in one country control over a company in another country – in this case, a Chinese company control over an enterprise in the US.

World FDI flows have grown from an average of $50 billion during the first half of the 1980s, to $2 trillion in 2007, before falling back to $1 trillion in 2009/10 as a result of the crisis.

Traditionally, the US has been the leading host and home country, i.e. the largest importer and exporter of FDI. Partly because of that, the US has traditionally been a leader in establishing a strong and open international investment law and policy regime (IILP regime) that protects FDI and even encourages it, with the principle of non-discrimination at its heart. The reason is that FDI can play an important role in strengthening the competitiveness of firms and in economic development.

This approach has gained widespread support from virtually all countries of the world and has led to a strong IILP regime. And, as I said, the US has always benefitted from this regime, being the largest host and home country. FDI has brought capital, employment and various other tangible and intangible assets to the US and helped the country's economic growth and development.

It is therefore surprising that there is so widespread skepticism regarding Chinese FDI in the US. This is all the more surprising since this investment in very small indeed: official data show that inflows were around $1 billion in 2009. (US flows to China that year were $3.6 billion, rising to $4.1 billion in 2010.) With total FDI inflows into the US amounting to $129 billion in 2009, China's share was less than 1% of the total.

However (and this is atypical if compared with other countries), some 80-90% of outward FDI flows from China are undertaken by state-owned enterprises (SOEs). At the same time, though, there is little if any systematic evidence that SOEs – be they headquartered in China, Singapore, France, Germany, or any other country – behave differently from private MNEs when they undertake FDI projects abroad.

The skepticism regarding Chinese FDI in the US appears to be reflected in the fact that the share of filings by Chinese firms with the Committee on Foreign Investment in the United States (CFIUS) is higher than the share of Chinese FDI in total FDI inflows into the US. And, of course, cases like the aborted takeover of UNOCAL by CNOOC received considerable attention in China.

It is of course true that Chinese firms face considerable challenges when establishing themselves in the US and operating foreign affiliates in that country that have little or nothing to do with any skepticism regarding Chinese FDI. Rather, they are the results of the inexperience of Chinese multinational enterprises (MNEs) – after all, they became active in the world FDI market in a significant manner only since 2000, when China launched its "going global" policy. Chinese MNEs, like all MNEs, face the "liability of foreignness" challenge, i.e. the challenge of a foreigner operating in a foreign market; for Chinese firms, this challenge is particularly high, given the regulatory and institutional differences and gaps between China and the US. Chinese firms simply do not have the experience of how to become quickly accepted in a host country, as good corporate citizens that contribute to the economic and social development of the communities in which they are established. This disadvantage can be further accentuated by the "liability of the home country", i.e. that Chinese firms having established themselves in the US may be regarded differently than, say, British firms that have done the same.

Mr. Chairman, let me conclude by offering four recommendations:

1. The US should strive to maintain its role as a leader in establishing a strong and open IILP regime to make sure that the rule of law governs FDI between countries. In particular, the principle of "non-discrimination", the heart of the IILP regime, should be respected and promoted. The China – US bilateral investment treaty that is under negotiation may offer an excellent opportunity to further strengthen this principle.

2. At the same time, I suggest that the IILP regime requires some rebalancing to allow governments to pursue their legitimate public policy objectives regarding their own essential security interests – or, more generally, their national interests. But an effort should be made to define or at least circumscribe these concepts as clearly as possible, to avoid that they are being used for protectionist purposes.

3. Outward FDI from China has grown rapidly and is likely to continue to grow. (China was, in 2009, the world's 5th largest outward investor.) The US should seek to attract as much of this investment as possible. (Naturally, efforts in this regard would meet stiff competition from other countries that seek to attract

the same investment.) The US should welcome Chinese FDI; at the same time, Chinese investors (like investors from other countries) need to observe strictly US laws and regulations. Such an approach – by the US and other countries – would also contribute toward the further integration of China into the world economy and making that country a responsible stakeholder in it.

4. Given that China's MNEs are young and inexperienced, we should find ways of helping them to become good corporate citizens – not only to avoid unnecessary frictions but also to increase the contribution of China's FDI to the US economy and society.

By way of conclusion, Mr. Chairman, let me remind us all that we had a similar situation some 25 years ago when Japanese firms emerged as major outward investors. Like today vis-à-vis Chinese firms, there was a strong reaction against the new kids on the block in light of a range of concerns. In fact, CFIUS was created at that time and in reaction to incoming Japanese investment. The US managed to integrate and accept Japanese FDI and, in fact, is actively seeking, it. I trust that, over time, we will have the same experience with Chinese FDI in the U.S.

Thank you very much for your attention.

PANEL IV: DISCUSSION, QUESTIONS AND ANSWERS

HEARING CO-CHAIR WESSEL: Thank you, both, for your thoughtful testimony and appearance here today.

I'd like to ask a question, Dr. Sauvant, and, Dr. Rosen, for your comment as well--regarding the last point you made. The last experience we had with concerns about foreign investment, foreign direct investment, in the United States, in the 1980s, the Japanese seeking to address some trade irritants and trade issues decided that investing here was to their advantage, both for the market but also to address, of course, some political issues. But in doing so, because they were advocates or proponents of just-in-time manufacturing and a number of other things, they brought their supply chains over with it.

So Toyota, Nissan and others over time built here the supply chain to support their U.S. facilities. As I look at, and for your comment, as I look at Chinese investments here, for example, the solar facility they're building in Arizona, to hire 1,000 employees, it's primarily a screwdriver facility. So that the bulk of the value that is going into those panels, solar panels, is going to be produced in China.

So as we've seen with brand acquisitions, because Chinese don't have international brands, with their foreign direct investment, the question is are we seeing a different quality of investment from what the Japanese did, that they are trying to create, if you will, indigenous demand for Chinese products that will create jobs here, which we welcome, but not as many as if they were truly following market forces and creating the supply chains that I think are being globalized day by day?

DR. SAUVANT: This is actually a very interesting issue and has found a lot of examination in the academic research. The result is that if you look at the typical internationalization path of a company, you find (at least in the past and to a large extent still today) that firms start by exporting, and then they start to establish maybe distribution facilities, then they start assembly facilities, precisely as you describe the Japanese as having done, and eventually they moved on to manufacturing.

The Japanese have long moved on to manufacturing. In fact, the concept of screwdriver investment was invented in the context of Chinese automobile investment in the United States that consisted of--

HEARING CO-CHAIR WESSEL: Japanese.

DR. SAUVANT: Japanese--excuse me.

HEARING CO-CHAIR WESSEL: Yes.

DR. SAUVANT: --assembly facilities in the United States. I would expect the same thing to happen on the Chinese side. In other words, they are testing the market. They are, to a certain extent, established through exports, either direct or as suppliers. I would expect that they more and more test the waters through assembly, distribution, and other investment. In fact, I understand that the biggest single foreign direct investment company from China in the U.S. is actually Cosco, which is a distribution or shipping company.

Now, can we encourage that process, can we speed it up? I guess we can. One of the things would be precisely to be more active in terms of attracting Chinese investment by pointing out where possibilities exist, where greenfield investment or perhaps even mergers and acquisitions are possible.

HEARING CO-CHAIR WESSEL: But China has for our investments, for example, as I recall, and the facts may be somewhat off, when GM created their facility in Guangzhou, as I recall, they made a commitment to source within five years 80 to 90 percent of the parts indigenously, and to, in fact, teach Chinese firms how to reach ISO-9000, 9001, and Sigma Six and all the various other requirements.

Should we have something similar here? I wish I had the faith that you do that the Chinese are going to follow the Japanese path of slowly migrating to creating their supply chains here. I fear that because they are a non-market economy, they are trying to create, if you will, the distribution centers, the assembly facilities, but the rest of the value chain is not going to come through.

Should we be taking actions to ensure that?

DR. SAUVANT: Well, the Japanese did not move on to full manufacturing because they wanted to do a favor to the United States. They moved on to full manufacturing because over time it became economically more sensible to manufacture here as opposed to manufacture in Japan and export to the United States.

Now as to the question of can one encourage Chinese firms that are established here to make an extra contribution to the economy by, for instance, establishing a local content requirement? Certainly not by making it mandatory, because that would violate the TRIMs Agreement under the WTO, but there may be other ways of doing that. For instance--and this is being done by a number of the countries that are members of the WTO and therefore subject to the TRIMs Agreement--instead of saying you must source locally, they encourage firms to source locally, for example, by making sure that foreign affiliates find appropriate suppliers that can produce at the cost and quality that foreign affiliates require. There are a number of programs that we can pursue in this respect. I think that is certainly something where in the U.S., at the state level and perhaps even at the federal level more could be done, and perhaps not only vis-a-vis Chinese firms, but others as well.

HEARING CO-CHAIR WESSEL: Dr. Rosen, for a very quick response or?

MR. ROSEN: I would only add to it that, you know, bear in mind the phenomenon you're talking about was what we called "tariff jumping" by the Japanese, in the 1980s, where they were coming here because they already were making a lot of money off us. Our tariffs threatened that, and that's the only reason they were coming over, and so they basically brought the family with them to keep doing the same thing.

Very few Chinese companies are coming to America for tariff-jumping reasons yet. We have a few cases that might be described that way. Mostly, it's because China is very weak economically at, say, three-fifths of the production chain. They're good in manufacturing as an OEM in the middle, which is a commoditized part of what we do to create value in the world today.

All the things that the profit margin is found in Cupertino and elsewhere, they don't do, which is why they're coming, and so it would be, wc have to be mindful not to over-extrapolate from the Japanese behavior in the '80s to what the Chinese will do in the years ahead.

HEARING CO-CHAIR WESSEL: Okay. Commissioner D'Amato.

COMMISSIONER D'AMATO: Thank you, Mr. Chairman. Thank you both for your testimony.

I'm particularly interested in the question of the adequacy of the screening process that you commented on. There are those who have come to us consistently knowing that the trend has been in the last ten years for larger and more powerful SOEs on the part of the Chinese that have, of course, a direct relationship with state policy coming to the United States.

We have a screening process, some say, that because it's voluntary, that those SOEs or those companies that might be interested in finding national security technologies and so on would be the ones that most likely would not voluntarily participate in the CFIUS process, and therefore we should have a mandatory CFIUS process.

Do you think that a mandatory process is egregious in general, or if it's an open process and there's no attempt to invade the national security arena, what would be wrong with an open process? I'm just wondering why you're saying--are you characterizing, recommending a mandatory process with politicization of that or is that simply just good governance to understand what it is that's coming in the country in terms of monitoring those things?

So I just wanted to clarify how you felt about that.

MR. ROSEN: Thank you, Commissioner.

Let me share my perspective on this. I think having the process be voluntary is advantageous from the perspective of the U.S. government and the United States. It places the burden on the Chinese investor to, you know, come to God with themselves about whether they are vulnerable to being unwound and shut down.

After they invest potentially billions of dollars in a transaction, they can be summarily kicked out of that investment and all that learning that they've transferred and everything they've done if they are in a sensitive area and they have not voluntarily asked for a stamp of approval from us.

If, on the other hand, we make it mandatory, then we have to investigate and certify every bubble gum factory and investment in a Dairy Queen that takes place in Peoria, and I don't think we necessarily want to do that.

The voluntary standard is only voluntary in that the company can choose to get precleared as not being in noncompliance. If they don't do that, then they are immensely vulnerable to what almost would feel like an arbitrary unwinding of their operations here.

So I don't think that the question of mandatory versus voluntary investigation of a Chinese investment prejudices the national security in that sense.

COMMISSIONER D'AMATO: Do you have a comment on that, Dr. Sauvant?

DR. SAUVANT: I just wanted to tell you a little anecdote. About two or three years ago when I was in China, I had a chance to meet with a fairly high level official of the Department of Commerce whose job was to attract investment to China. She got paid for that. And she said, you know, we are seeing CFIUS in the United States. If the United States as the most powerful country in the world, and the most powerful economy in the world, feels it has to screen foreign direct investment, what about us? Shouldn't we also look at incoming investment and see to what extent it helps us or hurts us?

And the same message, my guess is, is also sent to other countries. I'm not so much worried about that CFIUS might do something that may not be the proper thing, but I'm more worried about if other countries emulate the CFIUS model and other countries are doing it. China, in fact, earlier this year actually promulgated regulations establishing its own review process. That process may not be as clean as it is in the United States.

So I'm really wondering what kind of example the U.S. is giving in this area to the rest of the world.

COMMISSIONER D'AMATO: Thank you.

HEARING CO-CHAIR WESSEL: Commissioner Bartholomew.

COMMISSIONER BARTHOLOMEW: Thanks very much and thanks to both of our witnesses for appearing today, very thoughtful testimony.

A couple of comments, and then a question. My first comment, Dr. Sauvant, is that one of the differences between Japan and China, of course, is the size of the population. Japan has about 127 million people. What-- China is 1.3--teetering on 1.4 billion. They need to keep people employed, and they have a much greater number of people to keep employed than Japan ever did. So I think you need to factor that in when you think about will that old model fit.

A second point, and Dr. Rosen, this gets to something you were mentioning, which is narrative. The Chinese government, of course, builds its narrative as if they are the aggrieved party. And, frankly, I think certainly when dealing with the Americans, that provides them leverage.

The Chinese are choosing which leverage to go, which narrative to go with, in terms of their investment here in the United States, and they're going to get a whole lot more traction out of saying, "woe is us, you are not allowing our companies in," than if they said, "hey, this is fine."

I think you need to think about that as you think about narrative, but the point, the question actually I had, is that I want to go to this issue of the principle of nondiscrimination.

We have indeed had an international global regime where for the most part people have signed on to that idea. But what are we supposed to do when the second-largest economy in the world is not practicing that same thing? The analogy people like to say in different arenas is we're playing checkers and they're playing chess, and I just wonder how you see this all working out when we aren't even convinced that the Chinese government is interested in participating in the international economic regime under the same terms and conditions that other parties have?

DR. SAUVANT: Well, thank you for very interesting points. Let me just add another issue to the differences between Japan and China, apart from the size of the population and, therefore, the need to create employment, and, of course, part of this employment is being created through exports-- which incidentally I understand President Obama is also trying to do. So that's something which is common.

Perhaps what is equally important is also that, of course, the strategic relationship between Japan and the United States in the '80s was different from what is the strategic relationship as a potential competitor between China and the United States. So obviously one has to factor that in.

But, in the end, it comes down, at least to a large extent, I would argue, to the following question: do we believe what we have been preaching for 50 years, namely, that attracting foreign direct investment is good for you? It's good for you because it helps you to acquire capital, technology, skills, employment, exports and all the rest of it, and if that is true, if that still holds, then if another country says I don't want to attract investment, i.e., I like to shoot myself into foot, go ahead. It doesn't mean that we have to do the same thing.

So I think it really comes down to do we believe that foreign direct investment contributes to our development, both inward and outward foreign direct investment? Certainly what the Chinese seem to be doing more and more is that they are becoming much more selective in terms of saying that they want to have certain investment and give you special incentives for it. They also have a number of sectors, of course, which they say you are not allowed to invest in every country has such sectors. China has probably more sectors than others, but every country has its protected sectors. Then China has sectors that are open, and it has sectors in which it is encouraging foreign investment. And, of course, that means that the Chinese, too, agree that certain foreign direct investment—or actually most foreign direct investment--is beneficial to their own economy and economic development.

COMMISSIONER BARTHOLOMEW: Dr. Rosen.

MR. ROSEN: If I may, just to elaborate on the topic of narrative also, because it's really, it's the same point that Karl just rightly made. it has to do with what principles we believe we are defending, and where we get to the point where we say you know what, being a Boy Scout on this one is just going to get us killed, and so we're not going to be here tomorrow to debate this any longer, it's time to move on past that point of principle and be pragmatic in some way or another.

Well, most of the time there really is a choice to be made about which way we go; what kind of American economy we're going to have tomorrow?

Likewise, on the Chinese side, right now, there is a battle going on in Beijing for the soul of China's reform directions and the choices it make. Some people are saying we got where we got because we took a pretty liberal tact 30 years ago, and it's worked, and we were the most open emerging economy in the world to foreign direct investment.

And it meant our own guys got killed in competition, but we got rich doing that. We should stay that course. Others are saying look at what the Americans are doing, look at the way the world works, this got us 30 years, but it's time to take a different approach. Now, we consolidate the state's power in the economy and take advantage of that.

So the choices and the debates that are being held in Beijing right now are affected by what we do, by whether we're willing to stand by the principles we've developed and imbedded into the international system or not.

If we abandon ship of these kinds of liberal principles, I can assure you

113

it will not be missed in the debate taking place similarly in a hall like this in Beijing.

HEARING CO-CHAIR WESSEL: Commissioner Mulloy.

COMMISSIONER MULLOY: Thank you, Mr. Chairman, and thank you both for being here.

I want to put this in the context. I read an article by Warren Buffett in October 2003 in Fortune magazine, in which Warren Buffett said that the United States by running these massive trade deficits year after year is going to sell the country out from under itself.

His view was when you send out these dollars, they're claims on your economy, and they come back by purchasing our economy.

Secondly, my understanding, Professor, is we don't have a lot of rules, global rules, on investment. We have the TRIMs Agreement in the WTO. I know we tried at one point to get an OECD multilateral agreement on investment, but that failed. So there's not a lot of global rules that govern this system.

So countries can do pretty much what they want to do in regulating foreign investment. Is that correct?

DR. SAUVANT: The principal instruments governing foreign direct investment internationally are bilateral investment treaties, of which are about 2,700.

COMMISSIONER MULLOY: Yes, these are BITs. Those are not global rules. These are countries that are agreeing to these rules among themselves.

DR. SAUVANT: Otherwise you have the GATS agreement, but that only applies to services.

COMMISSIONER MULLOY: Right. Okay. So that's my understanding. So there really aren't WTO rules except for the TRIMs, and that's a very narrow thing. So countries can pretty much do what they want to do in this whole area unless they are tied up in these BITs, and we don't have a BIT with China; right?

DR. SAUVANT: Correct.

COMMISSIONER MULLOY: In our own CFIUS process, we make a distinction between government-owned companies buying here and private sector companies buying here, a more searching analysis when it's a government-owned company buying here.

And then we further understand that many of the companies coming here from China are either state-owned enterprises. How would you guys look at Huawei? Is that a private sector company or is that a government-owned enterprise or a government-influenced enterprise? What your take is on that.

Dan?

MR. ROSEN: We treat it as a private company. Our definition is if a firm has 80 percent or more private shareholding, we treat it as a private company even if there's up to 19.9 percent government shareholding.

In the case of Huawei, as you know, they claim that they're 100 percent employee-owned and have no government shareholding.

COMMISSIONER MULLOY: Right.

MR. ROSEN: So the question really becomes in the case of China, it doesn't even matter. Aren't all companies from China under the influence of the government of China, and they very much are to a greater extent than firms are here.

Exactly where you draw the line on government control may or may not be the useful thing to settle at the end of the day. But that's another subject. I don't mean to take up your time.

COMMISSIONER MULLOY: No, that's helpful. Now, my further understanding is that 90 percent of investment coming into the United States--and we're going to have a lot of it because we have a massive trade deficit. There are a lot of dollars out there which can now come back and buy assets. 90 percent of the investment coming to this country is acquisition investment; ten percent is greenfield.

Is that about what you understand the situation to be?

MR. ROSEN: I can speak to the China numbers.

COMMISSIONER MULLOY: No, I know you did that already. You said about half and half, I think. But my understanding, I was at a program the other day where an official from Commerce spoke, who was in charge of the investment; he said it was about 90 percent acquisition; ten percent greenfield.

DR. SAUVANT: Could be true.

COMMISSIONER MULLOY: Right? Okay. So it's not like it's adding new things. It's purchasing things that are already here that are now going to be owned by somebody else rather than here, and the profits then can go out of the country rather than stay here, which you ought to think about as well.

My understanding is that China has certain sectors of that economy that foreigners cannot own, so-called "pillar industries," and that these are large chunks of the Chinese economy.

Would you believe it's best to have a reciprocal investment policy rather than just we throw ourselves open and what they can wall off sectors of their economy? What's your impression of that, Dr. Rosen and then Dr. Sauvant?

MR. ROSEN: And for the record, my wife is Dr. Rosen. I'm a mere Mister.

COMMISSIONER MULLOY: Thank you.

MR. ROSEN: Well, Commissioner, as usual, provocative and important questions. I would say, and I believe, on the record, last time I was before the committee, I said that I would not embrace Communism if Communism were batting better in that inning.

And I continue to take that view, that things which appear strengths in

China today will come with a massive butcher's bill, which in a few years' time will change the story that we are currently engaged in.

I think marking China to market now and giving them a full credit for the performance of their economy today under state planning would be a mistake on our part. We should not, we should not do this transaction based on their current valuation.

We should consider where they might be in a few years from now and stick by our principal guns about capitalism, is where I am. As Karl put it, if somebody wants to bring bags of money and overpay for an asset in the U.S. or just pay a fair price, I'm willing to take it.

While 90 percent of the investment transactions may be M&A, remember that many of those are already owned by foreigners so they might entail a change of control by two foreign parties as in the Dubai Ports World case; right? It didn't entail a U.S. asset for the first time being held by parties abroad.

And then finally on this, in the Chinese case, one of the nice things about the Chinese data we have today is that there's a much greater propensity by the Chinese investor to do greenfield investment, in fact.

So those firms are not just buying existing assets. They're also building new facilities around the country. We'll see whether that reverts to the norm, as they say, and becomes more like the typical pattern we've seen from other investors as well, but there is some, there is some good positive aspects to the Chinese story as it's unfolding thus far, as well as the concerns which you rightly raise and which require much lengthier consideration.

COMMISSIONER MULLOY: Thank you.

DR. SAUVANT: If I may also comment on the very interesting observations. On the question of global rules, you're absolutely right, there are none apart from the TRIMs and the GATS Agreement.

But I would not underestimate the importance of the network of bilateral investment treaties and for that matter the additional 300 or so free trade agreements that have an investment chapter because they really involve all the big economies of the world, even if there is no bilateral treaty between the U.S. and China. I think we have the strongest international investment laws regime that we ever have had. That's one thing.

On the merger and acquisition question, if I had a choice to attract a greenfield investment or a merger and acquisition, as a rule, I would take a greenfield investment. No question.

But then it becomes more complicated. If the company I would take over is failing, maybe it's not bad if somebody else rescues it or if the foreign investor injects new technology, new export markets, and so on, it may make the company more profitable.

And, also, the money paid for the company that is being acquired, is presumably then released for investment in other parts of the U.S. economy or abroad. So after all, these are resources that can be used for other things. So I'm only saying that mergers and acquisitions, which are the predominant form of entry of foreign direct investment worldwide, do have also certain aspects to them which makes them desirable.

On the question of if the Chinese close certain sectors to foreign direct investment, should we do the same thing here, I have the same answer as before. If we think that foreign direct investment in certain areas is not good for us, then obviously we shouldn't let it in, let alone attract it.

But let's keep in mind that our policy with respect to the rest of the world and with respect to the U.S. has always been, and I would say for good reasons, that on balance, foreign direct investment helps economic growth and development.

COMMISSIONER MULLOY: Thank you.

HEARING CO-CHAIR WESSEL: Commissioner Shea.

COMMISSIONER SHEA: Yes. Dr. Sauvant, you forgot to mention that M&A investment in the United States also enriches U.S.-based lawyers and investment bankers, which is another positive thing, I suppose.

[Laughter.]

COMMISSIONER SHEA: Two obviously very intelligent individuals. Even though you might not have a doctorate, Mr. Rosen, but you're obviously a very smart man.

I have two questions. One, we have focused on potential U.S. barriers to foreign-direct investment. I would like you to both talk about what holds the Chinese back? Dr. Sauvant, you mentioned that they have a recognition that their managerial class may not be prepared to move out.

I also understand that every investment, proposed investment, by a Chinese company overseas has to get regulatory approval within China. I don't know if that is correct, but some sort of preapproval--if you could talk about that as a potential barrier.

And, then, finally, the other question I'd like to ask you--Mr. Rosen, you alluded to it at least--about the health of the Chinese economy. We had a little discussion this morning with Barry Naughton and Derek Scissors, and the notion was that there is such a misallocation of capital in the Chinese system. It's incredibly inefficient, and that the state dominance in the economy is ultimately unsustainable. I was just wondering if you have any comments on that?

MR. ROSEN: Thank you very much.

COMMISSIONER SHEA: Sure.

MR. ROSEN: Of course, companies going offshore creates almost as much work for U.S. lawyers as well. So they make money no matter what happens; right? Up market, down market.

In terms of what's holding Chinese companies back, well, the first part of my punch line that I want to make sure is driven home is that we can say that actually nothing is holding them back anymore. That the notion that's become ingrained that somehow the Chinese are being held at bay is not correct.

America is welcoming foreign investment, direct investment, and we're open to and welcoming of Chinese foreign direct investment in the United States; hence, it's growing 130, 150 percent year- over-year for years on years in a row now.

So that's the new story, and now it's time to understand why that's now happening and it wasn't happening before.

But we still are talking, you know, early days, and the things that still make it difficult for Chinese firms to do this are, first and foremost, as a senior Politburo official said to a Chinese company two years ago, you don't even speak Mandarin. He said this publicly to the CEO of the company. How the hell do you expect to go to the United States and speak English?

You don't even know what a sexual harassment lawsuit from an employee is. How are you going to go to America and try to do business?

So the cultural issues, the burden of operating in a heavily regulated, mature, sophisticated economy, where there is full tax reporting expected of you, and you don't keep two sets of books, that's no small burden, and the Chinese firms that have been able to make the jump so far are really, in many cases, to be lauded.

Harvard Business School is doing case study work on Wanxiang, for example, to understand how they're getting over these tremendous hurdles to doing business in America when their home market is so alien to the marketplace, to the marketplace here.

Just another ten seconds on the regulatory, outbound regulatory burden they face. Until two or three years ago, despite all the pronouncements about go global, there were big regulatory hurdles for Chinese firms getting the - especially the conversion of renminbi to dollars they needed to make outbound investments.

That, by and large, has been changed over to just a reporting requirement rather than a permission requirement. So up to, I think $100 million outbound investment now, Chinese firms are supposed to be able to just notify rather than get approval.

In practice, of course, if it's a state-related company, it's not going to get out of bed in the morning without making sure that that's what everybody expected them to be doing. But that's another part of the story.

DR. SAUVANT: I would also like to underline the importance of the lack of relative experience of Chinese companies in terms of international markets, and Dan has given some examples.

It's extremely difficult to make a merger and acquisition work. Think about it. Daimler Benz, not exactly one of the newest companies in the world, made a total mess out of its acquisition of Chrysler, and that was an experienced company.

So any Chinese firm--the CEO may not even be able to speak English--establishing itself in the United States, either through a greenfield investment or through a merger and acquisition, faces tremendous difficulties simply in terms of doing it and operating in this highly sophisticated and competitive environment.

In fact, one of the fears I have, given the climate, is that you have a major merger and acquisition by a Chinese firm going through, but then it goes busted. Everybody would jump on it and say, "you see"--and you fill in the dots. I think that is something where, again, we have a role to play, through our law firms, through seminars, through various mechanisms to help foreign companies, in this case, Chinese companies, really understand what it takes to operate here in the United States.

HEARING CO-CHAIR WESSEL: Thank you.

Chairman Reinsch.

CHAIRMAN REINSCH: Thank you.

I want to commend our panelists. I think you're both very wise. That is because you agree with me.

[Laughter.]

CHAIRMAN REINSCH: But in any event, I commend you on your wisdom. I think one of the things that's coming out here that you both made reference to is that it's probably useful for us to think carefully about how we proceed in this area because whatever we do to the foreigners is almost certainly going to be done to us.

Dr. Sauvant, you talked about the international regime, when it comes to control, these issues, TRIMs and what not. Can either or both of you comment on the extent to which or how many other countries or what other countries contain national CFIUS-like devices to control incoming investment?

Is this unique? This is not a unique phenomenon to the United States, I think.

DR. SAUVANT: Let me respond on two levels. If you look back 30 years or so, what you had in quite a number of countries were screening mechanisms for foreign direct investment, particularly in developing countries but also in a number of developed countries.

All of those were eventually turned into investment promotion agencies to do exactly the opposite. With the establishment of CFIUS in the late '80s, arguably, you could say that the trend is being reversed and we are going back to some screening because the example of CFIUS was followed by clarifications in Canada and in Australia; changes in the law in Germany, in France, in Russia; and now, well, China has its own approach toward reviewing mergers and acquisitions and a national security review.

So you have the reintroduction of screening mechanisms. What is ironic is that the United States, which had been the leader in liberalizing investment regimes and establishing a strong international investment law regime, has become the leader of sorts in terms of reestablishing some sort of screening.

I'm not too worried about what the United States does because it's being done maybe not in an entirely transparent fashion because you don't really know what's happening within CFIUS, but I think it's a fairly clean process. But I'm not so sure that other countries having the same or similar institutional set-up will also proceed in the same clean manner as the U.S. does.

CHAIRMAN REINSCH: That's a good point. Dan mentioned losing control of the narrative, if you will, earlier. This is an area where I think the narrative has also changed. For 40 years, the narrative was how can the United States best protect the interests of its investors overseas from expropriation, arbitrary treatment, seizure of assets, et cetera, et cetera?

Over the last few years, aided in part by sovereignty concerns that the Bush administration Justice Department had, the narrative has become how can we protect ourselves from the foreigners, which is a very different narrative.

And for people that are engaged in foreign, U.S. outward investment, and think it's win/win in terms of job creation here and there, it's kind of a disturbing trend in the narrative.

Let me ask a question also for Dr. Sauvant. One more. You had a very interesting explanation of the transition from exporting to sales operations, assembly facilities, manufacturing, and you used Japan as an example.

I think that's an apt example and a good narrative. It seems to me that the Japanese case, all that was compressed in a relatively short period of time, and I think, as my colleague here would probably agree, partly for political reasons. Do you see that time period being that short in the case of China?

DR. SAUVANT: That's difficult to say. But certainly I would advise, and I have done so, Chinese companies that seek to invest in the U.S.--and everybody wants to invest, everybody I speak to in China says we want to get into the United States market to take the Greenfield approach Also, there seems to be now a bit of an increase in interest to invest in Europe, apparently at least in part in reaction to incidents in which Chinese investment in the U.S. have been stymied.

I certainly advise any Chinese firm if it has a choice, to take the greenfield route as opposed to merger and acquisition. That's clear. Given the speed with which everything happens these days, I would expect that the process in the case of China in terms of moving from exporting to actually manufacturing in the U.S. might go faster, maybe not much faster, than the case of Japan.

CHAIRMAN REINSCH: Thank you.

DR. SAUVANT: It's strictly a guess.

HEARING CO-CHAIR WESSEL: Commissioner Wortzel.

COMMISSIONER WORTZEL: Dr. Sauvant, I really enjoyed your anecdote about the Chinese commerce official, and I'd like to give both of you two back.

I have an article in front of me from the Los Angeles Times, provided by our staff here, and there's an interesting story about Shanghai Jinjiang International Hotel, a state-owned company, buying joint ventures in hotels here in the United States.

I've been traveling in and out of China since 1979, lived there for five years, stayed in loads of Jinjiang Hotels as a military officer, as an academic, and I have never been in a Jinjiang Hotel where I wasn't given a room in the northeast quadrant of the hotel on an upper floor, and I have never been in an Jinjiang Hotel where I didn't have very heavy technical audio and video surveillance, and physical surveillance when I left my hotel, and where everything I brought with me wasn't searched.

Now, that says to me that there's an awful lot of cooperation going on between Chinese intelligence services and the staff of the Jinjiang Hotel. So I don't think that it's incendiary politicization if I feel that when I know Jinjiang is buying hotels in the U.S., the FBI begins to look at who Jinjiang is putting into the United States. I think that's prudent security concerns about the practices of Chinese intelligence and security services.

Second anecdote. I used to follow fairly closely the General Political Department of the People's Liberation Army. It has two objectives. One, generally U.S. policy, influencing U.S. policy toward Taiwan and checking on what Americans think about China.

So when the General Political Department formed a real estate company--it was called Kaili-- and Kaili Real Estate immediately opened offices in Atlanta, and within a very short period of time, suddenly, students from China and Taiwan at universities in Atlanta were being watched by people who worked for Kaili.

So I guess I'd say to you that that's two anecdotes, but if you are seeing a country with such deep influence over its citizens because it has this dominant single party, and you've observed practices like that, isn't it just prudent to take a little harder look at China than Japan, which was an ally and a member of CoCOM?

MR. ROSEN: I'm not sure if that was directed to me or Dr. Sauvant.

COMMISSIONER WORTZEL: It was not directed to anybody.

[Laughter.]

MR. ROSEN: You quoted back some of my verbiage about incendiary politicization so let me make a comment in response.

I understand your reaction to that characterization. However, in my remarks, you won't find anything that suggests in any way that we should lighten the scrutiny of Chinese investment in the United States.

In fact, as you know, Commissioner, the FBI would in no way ever be able to scour through a Jinjiang facility in China because it's in China, and the FBI can't do that.

I love the thought of having MSS- controlled assets in the U.S. subject to U.S. law enforcement, surveillance. It's against the law to privately spy on U.S. citizens without court authorization to do so.

So let's remember that the foreign direct investment screening process that we have evolved over the decades has a singular purpose: to identify specific national security threats. It is not meant to ensure that a company is going to obey U.S. national, state and local laws, regulations and code once they get here.

They are still obliged to do so. And espionage is very much against the law of the United States. That firm, if it were so easy to identify people tailing you coming out of Jinjiang Hotel in San Francisco, great, because we're going to round up an awful lot of assets very quickly and put them in U.S. jail.

So I think because there are so many other things that could be on the shoulders on the national security screening process, if we went down that road, I think we ought to expect it to do its part, which is to identify specific threats from a transaction, and then count on U.S. counterintelligence law and all the other things that we need to do to make sure that once the Chinese investors are here, they are not conducting espionage under the guise of commercial activity.

I feel, I, like yourself, but not to as great an extent, have every reason in the world to want and insist upon particularly careful scrutiny of Chinese investors in the United States.

DR. SAUVANT: I agree. I agree entirely with what Dan has said. All foreign investors have to obey by the laws and regulations of the United States, period. And that includes laws regarding espionage or anything else, and one has to keep a close eye on these matters.

To come back to my analogy with Japan, Japanese firms did not know much about nondiscrimination at the workplace, and one case actually went all the way to the Supreme Court. So what has to be done is to enforce the laws and regulations of the United States vis-a-vis all foreign investors, including, of course, Chinese.

HEARING CO-CHAIR WESSEL: Vice Chairman Slane.

VICE CHAIRMAN SLANE: Thank you.

One of the concerns that I have about Chinese foreign direct investment is that many Chinese companies have no or little source of capital expense, and let me give you an example. There's a company that was just started in China that is in the imaging business in which they are producing CAT scans, and the Chinese government funded the start-up of this company to the tune of $42 million.

The company had essentially no cost of capital. They now want to come into the United States and compete with General Electric and other companies that make imaging equipment in the United States. They told me that they are able to sell their imaging equipment at half the price of General Electric's, and their equipment is comparable.

These subsidies given by the Chinese government seem to give them such an unfair advantage to ultimately dominate these industries. Is that of concern to either of you?

MR. ROSEN: This is a really important question you ask. I'm awfully glad it came up. Traditionally, our stance as far as inward direct investment to the United States has been that if the investing party has preferential access to capital or something like that back home, that's all to the good for us. The seller of a U.S. asset is going to get overpaid or paid more than they would otherwise get paid by that.

The problem would arise if a country with a distorted cost of capital, let's say, were not just a price taker in the world market where he could use that advantage to snap up a few companies, but was so big that they were going to distort pricing worldwide and kind of poison the way that markets are supposed to function; right.

If that's where we're going, then indeed we have a profound sort of problem which our whole kind of jurisprudence and history around this issue has never really had to address.

The case of Japan, there were concerns about the cost of capital that Japanese firms enjoyed by virtue of the nature of Japanese corporate structures, but in the case of China, it's an even larger phenomena which some people are concerned might eventuate.

For the time being, as Dr. Sauvant and I pointed out, Chinese direct investment in the United States is less than one-tenth of one percent of the total. So in no way can Chinese inflows be said to be distorting the functioning of markets in America now.

Ultimately, if that, presumably for that company to continue to enjoy its advantage vis-a-vis American producers, they will be importing to the United States the CAT scanners they're making in China, and they would be, they would be vulnerable to dumping or CVD at that point.

If they somehow got their intermediate inputs here under antidumping barriers, under different tariff lines, and assembled them here, the screwdriver case, then we get into that discussion about whether that is ultimately going to screw up the offsetting positives from generally being open to Chinese investment.

DR. SAUVANT: This is actually a very interesting question, and it could be expanded into other directions, namely, to what extent one offers incentives to foreign investors to come in? But I think what might eventually be an answer to that issue, if it is indeed widespread or becomes more widespread, would be that one would have to see to what extent one could have a sort of international agreement rewarding subsidies, in this case not for trade but for foreign investment.

But it's highly tricky, and subsidies are not only given by the Chinese government to foreign investors, but by many European governments in all sorts of ways. And there is, as I mentioned, the question of to what extent do you subsidize inward foreign direct investment by actually providing all sorts of incentives?

The only problem is that when these issues were discussed in the WTO, or even in the OECD context, very few countries wanted to do anything about them because they wanted to keep their hands free in order to use incentives in both directions if and when they thought that would make sense.

HEARING CO-CHAIR WESSEL: Are there any other questions on the first round? If not, we have three for the second round, and since we only have a couple minutes left, if they could be very quick.

Commissioner Bartholomew, myself, and Commissioner Mulloy.

COMMISSIONER BARTHOLOMEW: Yes, I think it's probably more of an observation than a question this time around, but it seems to me, and this won't surprise my esteemed Chairman at all, that I actually disagree with him. And it strikes me as interesting that we are supposed to--

CHAIRMAN REINSCH: Oh, I'm shocked.

HEARING CO-CHAIR WESSEL: Chairman of the Commission, not the chairman of the panel.

COMMISSIONER BARTHOLOMEW: Yes--that we are supposed to accept the idea that what we do to them, they will do to us, but that we aren't allowed to accept or supposed to accept the concept that what they do to us, we will do to them, which, of course, is at the heart of a lot of this nondiscrimination we're talking about or reciprocity that we're talking about.

But for me there's a fundamental question about the paradigm. I think you both accept this paradigm that the way things have worked in the past on trade, they will work in the future. But I think when you have to look at the facts on the ground, that it's not working for the hundreds of thousands of American people who have lost their jobs because of the way that this global trade regime has been defined.

And, Mr. Rosen, I think we probably disagreed ten years ago. We very well might disagree ten years from now, but I think what troubles me a little bit listening to both of you is there's a distinction between the way things should work and the way things are actually working.

I guess I would say if you can address that there's a difference between theory and practice, and what I am really concerned about is the outcome, the results on the ground.

MR. ROSEN: Let me just say, because it is one reason why I embraced the opportunity to be with you today, that the singular objective of this piece of work that I previewed, which will be out in a month or so, is to accurately illustrate what's happening on the ground in real terms, that the issue you're grappling with as Commissioners, what's the significance of

Chinese direct investment in the United States, you have no idea. You have no idea. You are operating in the dark right now.

I promise you and I assure you that that's what you are doing. The best that you might have is data from 2008, which partially captures some of what China did previous to that year for the most part.

I am quite dedicated, in fact, to using the best available quantitative and qualitative methods to shine greater light on the actual trends taking place in the marketplace today in terms of real concrete investments in America.

You've got concerns with the global trading system, and I share some of them, in fact. For today, though, I really was confining the implications of my remarks not to the global trading system but to Chinese direct investment, M&A and greenfield, in the United States.

COMMISSIONER BARTHOLOMEW: That's fair.

DR. SAUVANT: If I may make just a very quick comment on your observation that hundreds of thousands of Americans have lost their job or have no job. In order to change that, the only way is more investment. If you get the investment from at home, absolutely fine. But if not, then I think you should take it from abroad: the investment dollar from China is as green as the investment dollar from France, provided everybody works within the system and applicable laws and regulations.

The bottom line of that is, and I go back to something that Dan also said, that the U.S. should make a bigger effort to attract investment from abroad, in general, and including China. That's where the investment is coming from. During the crisis, world investment flows declined by 50 percent. Outward investment from China remained level, and it will increase. That's where the investment dollars are. If U.S. is not going to get it, the Europeans are going to get them, and others will get them. They'll be happy if you scare the Chinese away.

COMMISSIONER BARTHOLOMEW: Thank you.

HEARING CO-CHAIR WESSEL: Thank you, gentlemen.

Mr. Rosen, we are looking forward to your discussion, your paper coming up. I can assure you we do look at this very carefully. We are not traveling in the dark, and there are a lot of facts and specific circumstances which economists are not necessarily aware of. So the trends you refer to do not always identify all the facts and specific instances.

I want to question whether there's a fundamental disconnect here because what you two are talking about and others have talked about is based on economic theory that relies on market forces. We heard earlier today on the SOEs in terms of the size of their involvement in the Chinese market. Many of the companies coming here, and you both identified the trends, coming here are state-owned, state-invested, state-influenced entities, and China is not a market economy.

So they are not responding by definition to all the market forces/all the market signals that one would expect. It seems we're all hoping that China will be like us, but the trends over the last three years are for the strengthening of the state sector, not weakening, not their greater response to market forces, but just the exact opposite.

We see firms like Huawei and others coming here that are heavily subsidized, are state-controlled, even though they profess private ownership, and our security officials are responding appropriately to make sure that we have the proper screen. We want the foreign investment, but we should have some kind of scrutiny as it relates to governmental control and governmental involvement. This is not market-based investment, the large portion that's coming here.

Can you respond to that, the market signal issue?

DR. SAUVANT: Well, if I may start, very briefly, yes, one needs, at least to a certain extent, a mechanism that exercises some scrutiny concerning state-controlled entities that invest abroad. But it needs to be done in a nondiscriminatory manner, in other words, not only regarding China but also everybody else.

HEARING CO-CHAIR WESSEL: Singapore, Vietnam, you name it.

DR. SAUVANT: And so on.

HEARING CO-CHAIR WESSEL: Yes.

DR. SAUVANT: Yes. And if it is done--and this is where I see the biggest problem--if it is done within a framework which is clearly defined so that it cannot be misused for other purposes, especially protectionist purposes.

It's extremely difficult, of course, to establish such a framework, but it is needed because otherwise the predictability which the current international investment law regime provides will be impaired, and nobody benefits from that, least alone the United States.

One more thing about the possibility that state-owned enterprises act potentially on political impulse more than on commercial impulse. This seems to be something that one would expect on the face of it, at least to a certain extent, never mind whether state-owned enterprises are Chinese state-owned enterprises or French or German ones. But show me a few cases where a state-owned enterprise undertook a greenfield investment or a merger and acquisition that wouldn't have been made by a privately-owned enterprise in the same industry. In other words, what I am saying, is it's extremely difficult to show, and certainly for a number of cases, that state-owned enterprises are following political objectives as opposed to commercial objectives. On the surface, one would think so, but where is the evidence?

HEARING CO-CHAIR WESSEL: Commissioner Mulloy.

COMMISSIONER MULLOY: Thank you, Mr. Chairman, and thank you, again, both for being here.

An observation first. The United States at one point was the largest creditor nation in the world, and we were looking to invest abroad, and we pushed these open investment regimes. The United States because it's run massive trade deficits year after year is now the largest debtor nation in the world, and that title is fast increasing because we're continuing to run massive trade deficits year after year.

So those dollars that are out there are claims on the American economy, and they can go back and buy portions of our economy.

Mr. Rosen, you say on page one of your testimony that you're going to talk about direct investment, and that's that very small portion you talk about.

There's also portfolio investment. China now has a sovereign wealth fund, which is a government-owned hedge fund essentially, which can buy chunks of American companies. My understanding is they bought about ten percent of Citibank, ten percent of J.P. Morgan, and ten percent of Morgan Stanley.

We've traditionally not wanted our own government owning big portions of the American economy, and that's why we're all upset that the Obama administration somehow ended up owning GM. I know that Mr. Cox when he was Chairman of the SEC talked about this problem. And he testified on sovereign wealth funds as being different. Mr. Bremmer has written a very interesting book about state capitalism, makes the same point.

Can a foreign government when it owns ten percent of a very influential political entity like J.P. Morgan, can that buy political influence in this country in terms of how we perceive of a lot of these issues? That's a new worry that some people have. I want to get your judgment on that. Is that something we should be worried about?

MR. ROSEN: So the CIC transactions that you spoke of are classed as portfolio investment in the United States. They came up at 9.9 percent or so ownership stakes, intentionally stayed south of the ten percent threshold so they would not be direct investments.

On the other hand, CIC last year took a greater than ten percent stake in AES Energy in the U.S. energy and infrastructure space south of the river in Virginia. That is a direct investment.

In all those cases, in both sets of cases, however, direct and indirect, CIC is investing in an extremely passive manner. If they knew how to be a direct investor in the United States, then they would work more independently. They are far more inclined to provide mandates to manage some of the dollars they've been tasked with putting to work to U.S. investment companies to help them do that.

There is, of course, the concern and danger that a sovereign wealth fund might try to, in addition to delivering a positive return on investment so that it's not embarrassed back home for squandering the country's wealth, which is CIC's real anxiety that keeps it up at night, that somehow a government might to try to express some political intention through the fund managers who used to work on Wall Street and got recruited back to Beijing to staff CIC. That's extremely difficult to imagine that conspiracy to be an agent of influence in Washington working its way in through CIC's behavior.

Nonetheless, it's a concern. There are agents of foreign influence law. Again, I come back to not trying to ask the poor fellows on CFIUS to anticipate how an organization that might be government-related will behave in the future, but instead let's make sure we screen for discrete national security risks, and then we have domestic law, including national security law domestically, that monitors the behavior of foreign entities here to make sure they don't behave in a manner disadvantageous to the United States.

HEARING CO-CHAIR WESSEL: Thank you.

COMMISSIONER MULLOY: Thank you both.

HEARING CO-CHAIR WESSEL: That's the end of today's hearing. I want to thank our staff, Paul, Nargiza and Lauren, for their help in setting this up--and others who were involved. We appreciate it, and we stand adjourned until our next hearing barring a government shutdown.

[Laughter.]

[Whereupon, at 2:37 p.m., the hearing was adjourned.]

***

ADDITIONAL MATERIAL SUBMITTED FOR THE RECORD

STATEMENT BY MICHAEL H. MICHAUD, A U.S. REPRESENTATIVE FROM THE STATE OF MAINE.

Thank you for inviting me to testify today before the U.S.-China Economic and Security Review Commission. I am pleased that your hearing today will focus on the difficulties of competing against China's state-owned enterprises (SOEs). This is an important topic that has very real local impacts in Maine and throughout the country.

Before I begin my testimony, I want to suggest that we look at the issue differently. It's not just state-owned enterprises in China that American companies have trouble competing against. The Chinese government uses subsidies and interest free loans, among other things, to promote scores of companies and industries that aren't technically state-owned enterprises. But the effect of these subsidies is the same. So my recommendation to the Commission is to not focus on just those companies that are explicitly state-owned, but take a broader view of state-promoted enterprises in China.

I believe combating China's trade violations, especially their promotion of specific companies and sectors, is critical to our economic recovery as well as our national security. And we must respond to their unfair trade practices by focusing on our manufacturing sector at home and aggressively combating their trade fraud abroad.

My thoughts on China's role in the global economy and the American economy have been shaped by the negative impacts China's unfair trade practices have had on Maine's communities. Our paper industry, for example, has felt the consequences of China's decisions to become a global leader in paper products. Domestic mills simply can't compete against companies that get interest free loans or enormous subsidies. I think it's important to state that often these companies aren't state-owned enterprises, but the favorable treatment they get from Beijing often makes them an equally big threat to American companies.

But it's important to note here, that the single biggest challenge from China facing American companies is the undervaluation of the yuan. All questions about how we should respond in the face of state-owned enterprises are moot unless we address China's currency manipulation. Congress must pass the Currency Reform for Fair Trade Act immediately, and President Obama must sign it into law. In addition, the U.S. should bring a WTO case against China for undervaluing its currency. Their currency manipulation puts Americans out of work and forces American businesses to close their doors. We must act with urgency to stop it.

Maine's paper companies got some relief at the end of last year when the International Trade Commission made a positive determination and the Department of Commerce began levying duties on certain Chinese and Indonesian paper imports. These tariffs helped the Maine firms rebound, and some of them were able to hire back workers as a direct result. This response proved two important things: first, that American companies can compete successfully on a level playing field; and second, that we must use all of the tools at our disposal to try to bring China in line.

But this won't be easy. China's national policies often violate international trade law. For example, several years ago, China decided that it wanted to be the global leader in paper products and embarked on a strategy of illegal trading practices to achieve this goal. They were successful; in 2008, China – despite having no lumber natural resources to speak of – became the world's largest producer of paper products. Such laser-focused and at-all-costs plans are typical of China's government. And this presents the main challenge Congress and communities all across America face: How do you respond to and engage economically with a country that so flagrantly violates international rules?

I am not sure there is a way to engage economically with China that will protect our workers and businesses from their nefarious trade practices. Congress wrestled with this issue when they were deciding in 2000 whether or not to give China Normal Trade Relation status. At that time, the proponents argued that admitting China into the WTO would allow us to better engage them and respond to their unfair trade practices. Although we will never know what would have happened if we had not admitted them into the WTO, it seems clear that letting them into the global trade framework has not resulted in their compliance with international trade law. So what do we do now? I think we have to develop and devote resources to two important strategies.

The first would be a national manufacturing sector strategy. If China is going to implement nation-wide policies designed to boost specific sectors, we must fight fire with fire. Our strategy should not involve illegal subsidies, but it should involve clear objectives. We should ask ourselves the question: what should the American manufacturing sector look like? I believe a diverse, robust manufacturing sector is key to a strong American economy and critical to our national security. The strategy should also evaluate what policy changes are needed to promote more domestic production. Seeking input from companies that currently choose to make their products in the U.S. would help to develop these ideas. We should consider ways to incentivize U.S. production through our tax structure. And finally, the manufacturing strategy should establish clear metrics of success over the short-, medium-, and long-term. Our manufacturing sector has declined over several decades, and it won't be rebuilt overnight. But if we are going to compete against China's state-owned enterprises, or the industries that receive preferential treatment by Beijing, we are going to have to have our own roadmap for the U.S. manufacturing industry.

The second strategy we must develop is a comprehensive trade enforcement strategy. The USTR under the Obama Administration has already taken strides to enforce our trade laws and keep China in line. But they do not have enough resources, and the trade enforcement tools are not accessible to enough American companies. In 2010

USTR filed three WTO disputes with China. Surely this is a small fraction of China's WTO violations. The problem is that initiating WTO disputes is extremely time- and resources-consuming. The same is true for anti-dumping and countervailing duty cases at the Department of Commerce and the ITC. Only seven anti-dumping and countervailing duty cases were filed last year, all of them against China. Our trade enforcement strategy must increase the resources available to USTR, the Department of Commerce, and the ITC to investigate and analyze the petitions submitted to them. In addition, we must find a way to make these tools available to smaller companies who cannot hire law firms to put together a petition or cannot afford to collect all of the data necessary to make their case that China's unfair trade practices are putting them out of business.

These two strategies should be pursued as matters of economic development and national security. We cannot sit idly by while China out-produces and out-grows the U.S. economy. Instead, we must look at our own economic priorities and adjust them accordingly. I firmly believe that a strong, diverse manufacturing sector is key to maintaining our spot as the global economic leader. Congress and the Administration must devise a comprehensive strategy to rebuild our manufacturing sector. We cannot compete against China's illegal trade practices without one. We must also work to make our trade remedies available to more Americans. Although I do not believe the WTO is always the most effective means of getting China to play by the rules, I do believe we must give every affected American company the opportunity to file a formal complaint against China's violation of their WTO commitments.

And we must address China's currency manipulation. The time for diplomacy is over. Congress and the Administration must act now to stop China from undervaluing the yuan. We can't afford not to – American jobs and our economic viability are at stake.

Thank you for the opportunity to participate in today's important hearing.

ADDITIONAL MATERIAL FOR THE RECORD from ROBERT E. SCOTT:

Manufacturing job loss: Productivity is not the culprit

Snapshot for February 21, 2007.

Manufacturing job loss: Productivity is not the culprit

The United States lost 3.1 million manufacturing jobs between 2000 and 2006. Despite reasonably strong GDP growth over the past three years, manufacturing employment has not recovered. There is a widespread misperception that rapid productivity growth is the culprit for continuing job loss in the sector.

Employment growth in any economic sector is essentially the difference between growth in output and productivity (output per hour). Output growth, all else equal, spurs employment while productivity growth dampens it. The figure below illustrates why manufacturing employment has fallen so rapidly over the last three years.

Between 1989 and 2000, manufacturing output and productivity growth averaged, respectively, 3.5% and 3.9% per year. As a result, the two largely offset one another and manufacturing employment was relatively stable, as shown in the figure. Since 2000, productivity growth nudged slightly upward relative to the previous decade, increasing 4.2% per year. Output growth, however, cratered, and has averaged only 0.8% per year since 2000. Employment fell 3.2% per year as a result. In short, it is slow growth in manufacturing output—not an acceleration in productivity—that makes 2000-06 different from the previous decade and explains the steep fall in manufacturing employment.

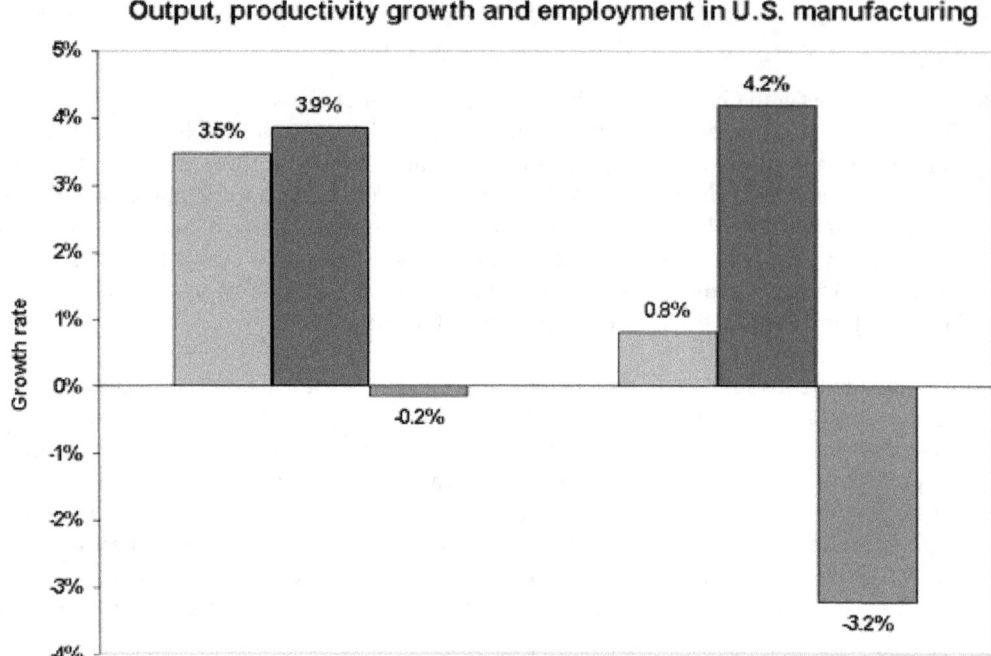

Output, productivity growth and employment in U.S. manufacturing

Source: EPI analysis of Bureau of Labor Statistics data

http://www.epi.org/economic_snapshots/entry/webfeatures_snapshots_20070221/